PETER BRABHAM

BARRY

THE HISTORY OF THE YARD AND ITS LOCOMOTIVES

An imprint of
Ian Allan Publishing

'In 20 or 30 years from now they'll be amazed to hear how engines from Barry were saved. If there is a word to sum it up, it's "magic".'

DAI WOODHAM, MAY 1989

This book is dedicated to:

All the thousands of miners killed in the pursuit of coal in South Wales

The 150 men killed in the construction of Barry Docks

Mr Dai Woodham MBE BEM (1919-1994)

and

The hundreds of men and women who have renovated the Barry locomotives

First published 2013
Reprinted 2013
ISBN 978 0 86093 643 5

© Peter Brabham 2013

Published by Oxford Publishing Co

an imprint of Ian Allan Publishing Ltd, Hersham, Surrey KT12 4RG.
Printed in England by Short Run Press, Exeter.

Visit the Ian Allan Publishing website at www.ianallanpublishing.com

Distributed in the United States of America and Canada by BookMaster Distribution Services

Contents

FRONT COVER TOP GWR 'King' class No 6023 *King Edward II* is captured on shed at Cardiff Canton depot on 18 February 1962. No 6023 was withdrawn in June of that year and by a series of fortunate coincidences arrived subsequently at Barry scrapyard. *John Wiltshire*

FRONT COVER BOTTOM The deteriorating condition of GWR No 6023 *King Edward II* in Barry scrapyard is obvious on 2 September 1978. Note the graffiti on the locomotive, giving up hope of ever restoring this once magnificent locomotive. *Albyn Austin*

BACK COVER After 22 years of deterioration standing in the salty sea air at Woodham Brother's scrapyard Barry, followed by 27 years of restoration, GWR No 6023 *King Edward II* makes its official relaunch back to steam at the Great Western Society, Didcot on 2 April 2011 – a magnificent effort of heritage preservation. *Peter Brabham*

PAGE 1 The amazing spectacle of over 200 rusting steam locomotives lined up in the Main Yard of Woodham Brothers scrapyard site at the western end of Barry Docks, circa 1967. *Peter Brabham collection*

Introduction

I was born in the early 1960s in the Rhondda Fawr Valley in South Wales, close to the location where in 1864 David Davies of Llandinam famously struck a rich seam of steam coal at Maindy colliery. This discovery radically changed this small part of the world forever and also drastically influenced my own personal family history. Without this geological discovery, I would probably be a farmer in North Devon, or a policeman in rural Gloucestershire, not the grandson of a Welsh coal miner. I do not come from a family of railwaymen and have no personal recollections of working British Railways steam locomotives, as they had by 1964 been replaced in the South Wales valleys by diesels. However, I have memories of the many small industrial locomotives busy shunting in the various colliery sidings, particularly at Mardy, Pontypridd and Maesteg well into the late 1970s.

In my youth, regular visits to the sea-side usually involved trips to the Gower, Porthcawl or Barry Island. My father, who was a mining engineering lecturer, liked visiting Barry Island in particular, because after playing cricket on the beach with my brother, we would then pay a visit to climb on the abandoned steam engines in the docks. My father was particularly fond of pointing out the great Bulleid Pacific locomotives with West Country names such as *City of Wells* and the 'Battle of Britain' locomotives such as *Tangmere*. He would also point out the Great Western 'King' and 'Castle' locomotives that used to pull the 'Red Dragon' expresses from Cardiff to London. Being a keen photographer, I would take photographs of the locomotives using my Kodak instamatic camera. These scrapyard visits influenced my brother's choice of career, as he now fixes London Underground's tube trains and also by serendipity looks after the LT Museum's working heritage stock including a working steam locomotive.

On attending comprehensive school in 1973, my train-spotting friend Simon persuaded me to join the 71000 Duke of Gloucester Preservation Society and we both travelled down to Barry by DMU to help with restoration work parties. This activity only lasted one summer until the *Duke* was taken off to Loughborough in April 1974. The lifting of the UK steam ban in the early 1970s also meant that the Great Western Railway's magnificent *King George V* was often captured running between Newport and Hereford. Then for a while steam locomotives took a backseat as for the next few years Simon and I became more interested in travelling the UK by train, 'copping' 'Westerns' and 'Deltics'. By the late 1970s the established heritage steam railways such as the Severn Valley, North York Moors, Keighley & Worth Valley, Bluebell and Torbay Steam Railway were the focus of many family holidays. In my teens I joined a local camera club with my Zenit EM camera and learnt how to develop and print black and white film. For the 1979 camera club competition I undertook a photo assignment with my new Canon AE-1 to photograph the remaining Barry scrapyard locomotives using grainy Ilford film but only won a commended prize. I was in awe of the superb technical imagery of Eric Treacy, Ivo Peters, R. J. Blenkinsop, the more atmospheric imagery of Ian Krause, Colin Gifford, Paul Riley and the total genius of O. Winston Link.

In my later teenage years I lost interest in railways, becoming more interested in physics and playing sport. In 1979 I attended Cardiff University to read geophysics and had by then pretty much forgotten about my past interest in railways, except for the old slides and negatives stored away in my mother's attic. In 1983 I won a PhD award to study coal exploration techniques at Durham University and spent four happy years exploring the north east of England. On weekends I would drive over to the Yorkshire Dales where I discovered the delights of the Settle & Carlisle Railway and also rediscovered railway photography. For a few years I had a good deal with my friends Tim and Fred from the Durham University Climbing Club. They would pay the £10 petrol cost and I would drive them in my Morris Marina to a remote Yorkshire Dales crag and drop them off, while I would spend a day taking photographs and pick them back up on the way home. This mutual arrangement allowed me to chase *City of Wells*, *Duchess of Hamilton* and *Union of South Africa* and others to Ribblehead, Newcastle, York, Knaresborough and Scarborough with my newly-acquired large format Yashicamat 124G.

A PhD qualification in coal exploration in the 1986 post-miner's strike Thatcherite era offered few industrial career opportunities. I thus landed a one-year teaching and research job in Cardiff University and have been there ever since. For weekend recreation throughout the late 1980s and 1990s, I would often combine a day out with my wife Anne with the interception of a mainline steam special or a visit to a heritage steam railway with my Canon A1 and second-hand Mamiya RB67. Later many holidays with my young family were strategically located near to Whitby, Swanage or Paignton for obvious reasons. My brother's connections also gave me an inside track on London Transport's 'Steam on the Met' events. Gradually, one by one, ex-Barry locomotives were being restored back to steam throughout this era, some to mainline standard, so there was often something new to photograph. Apart from the odd photograph in a railway magazine, my photography was purely recreational. I also paid visits to Barry scrapyard, but by the late 1980s it was a fairly dismal place with only the remaining shells of ransacked locomotives daubed in paint.

The genesis of the idea for this book came from two independent directions. After a merger within Cardiff University I was brought together in a professional capacity with marine and bus author Andrew Wiltshire. Andrew and I soon realised we had mutual interests in photography and transport. Andrew's father John is a prolific and gifted photographer and has a large collection of largely unpublished images from the 1950s onwards, including the early Barry scrapyard years. This book is partially a vehicle to get many of John's superb railway images out there for people to enjoy, as they chart the decline of steam and the scrapyards of South Wales in colour-rich Kodachrome. Secondly, in 2008 my professional research into the geophysical mapping of derelict land brought me back to Barry Docks and the area of Woodham Brother's sidings which was now under a major redevelopment plan. I use this dockland development site as the case study training area for my Masters' course. Students study archive air photography to estimate the type and location of ground contamination present, prior to designing invasive ground investigations. For this exercise I started to acquire a library of historical photographs of the docks site, many of which had been tucked away in archives and have not been published.

The publishers Ian Allan approached Andrew Wiltshire about a book on Barry scrapyard locomotives, but he was fully occupied writing about tugs and buses. Andrew suggested that I could write such a book by combining my photographs with his and also his father's collection. This seemed like a great idea at the time, but it has resulted in over three years of cataloguing, researching, digitally scanning and image processing many hundreds of slides and negatives in my 'spare time'. It also involved a steep learning curve on how to best digitally restore 40-50-year-old negatives and slides in various states of deterioration. It soon became apparent that key images of certain locomotives were still missing even after combining our collections and I am very grateful to the other photographers who subsequently loaned me many superb images of Barry scrapyard in the 1960s and 70s and a few preserved locomotives to fill in the storyline. Many of these photographers with scrapyard collections became aware of the book project through the 67-member Barry scrapyard group I set up on the FLICKR photographic website.

I wanted the book to take a larger chronological view of the scrapyard, in the context of the reasons for the rapid development and decline of Barry docks and railways within South Wales' larger industrial history. The questions therefore are: why were more than 200 steam locomotives allowed to stand derelict for over 20 years, why was Woodham Brothers the only scrapyard in the UK not to actually scrap its locomotives, how and when the locmotives got there, where they came from and what eventually happened to them? If in future while on holiday you visit a heritage steam railway in deepest rural England or northern Scotland and overhear somebody say 'that's a Barry locomotive', you will now know what that means. Strangely the 21st-century success of Britain's standard gauge heritage lines owes a lot to a Welsh scrap merchant and the availability of a large tract of derelict land at a South Wales port. Sadly however no working restored Barry locomotive has found a home in South Wales, which is a tragedy for an area so rich in Britain's industrial history.

I trust you enjoy this book which chronicles the 128-year history of Barry docks, the 30-year history of Woodham Brother's scrapyard and the subsequent 22 years since its closure. Barry Woodham Brother's scrapyard fuelled the growth of Britain's heritage railways by supplying steam locomotives for preservation (some projects are still on-going), restored to working order by a few wealthy individuals and by the thousands of unpaid volunteer enthusiasts throughout the UK; it is quite a remarkable story.

Acknowledgements

First and foremost I would like to thank John and Andrew Wiltshire for allowing me access to their personal well-indexed photographic collections. I would also like to thank my brother David for loaning me his collection of negatives. In the course of researching this book I have become friends with John Woodham and John Wynn, and thank them greatly for their personal memories of Barry scrapyard and providing access to their family scrapbooks. Roger Hardingham and the late Martin Beckett are responsible for the definitive 'Barry list' which is an invaluable and definitive source of reference. I also thank Michael Peter Waller and Nick Grant of Ian Allan for editing my electronic files into the final printed book format.

For helping greatly with the historical research, I thank the staff at the Air Photo Unit of the Welsh Assembly Government Cardiff, Royal Commission for Ancient Monuments in Wales, Ordnance Survey, the archivists at the National Waterfront Museum Swansea, the library staff at Cardiff University and Barry Town libraries.

The following photographers have contributed their personal images and collections to the production of this book :

Chris Aldred, Albyn Austin, Dave Bowles, Chris Boyd, Ian Bowskill, David Brabham, Peter Brabham, Class 20 Society, Paul Chancellor (Colour-Rail), the late Hedley Davies, Richard Fox, Rod Mckay, Chris Ravenscroft, the late Les Ring, Barry Smith, Alan Stoddern, Gordon Thompson, John Woodham, David Woodward, Andrew Wiltshire, John Wiltshire and John Wynn.

A number of original slides have been purchased by Peter Brabham where the original photographer's name is unknown. These images are credited as being the author's collection and the original unknown photographers are also thanked greatly for contributing to this book project.

Lastly thanks to my long-suffering wife Anne and daughters Helen and Sarah for putting up with many visits to heritage railway lines and for allowing dad to disappear off into his attic office for many hours at a time.

Peter Brabham

Setting the scene: Barry Docks, the railway and the island

Setting the scene

The story of one of the most remarkable episodes in British Industrial heritage preservation begins in the late 19th century with a small beautiful limestone island with a stunning sandy beach called Whitmore Bay, located off the South Wales coast in the Bristol Channel. The estuary between the mainland and the island was subject to large tidal changes, as the Bristol Channel has the second largest tidal range in the world. At low tide visitors could cross to the island using a shallow ford.

Archaeological evidence indicates that the island had probably been occupied by Iron Age, Bronze Age, Roman and Viking people throughout its history. In 1188 there was an ivy-covered chapel with the supposed remains of the 6th-century Celtic St Baruch, and it is from this saint that Barry is reputed to get its name. In 1191 the famous writer Giraldus Cambrensis (Gerald de Barry) described Barry Island in his writings, and his family name of De Barry was derived from their ownership of Barry Island. Barry also has a small 14th-century castle, which was plundered by Owain Glyndwr in 1402. From the 16th century onwards, the island had a small harbour, which traded in the Bristol Channel and was also the port for the hill town of Llantrisant. Local lead ore was traded with the glass-makers of Bristol. Local mythology also likes to envisage the island as a haven for the 18th-century Bristol Channel smugglers.

By the 19th century Barry was a very small village, with a population of only 70 people. Nearby were the small villages of Cadoxton and Porthkerry, with a total population, including Barry, of fewer than 500 people living in small scattered farmhouses. At this time the location was rather idyllic, with small fishing boats resting on the shingle of the old harbour, and trading between Barry and the North Somerset coastal villages. In 1856 Barry Island was sold for £3,200 to Francis Crawshay of Merthyr, and he built the

Marine Hotel where groups of Victorian travellers would cross the tidal estuary by a ferry boat at high tide. Crawshay then sold the island to Captain Jenner in 1867 for £10,000, who in turn sold it on to chemist and coal owner John Treharne in 1873 for £7,200. Both Jenner and Treharne had ambitious ideas about developing the tourist potential of the island and promoted the unsuccessful Barry Harbour Act of 1866. In 1867 Jenner proposed a direct railway over to the island for tourists, by means of a 150-yard wooden-piled bridge incorporating a swing bridge. He did, however, build a pier on the island, which was visited by paddle steamers. In 1877 Treharne and partners obtained an Act to build a railway extension from Penarth to Barry, although his plans were unfulfilled, and he sold the freehold of the island in 1878 for £12,500 to Lady Clive, who conveyed it to her son as his 21st birthday present. Her son became Lord Windsor, later Earl of Plymouth. In 1878 the Windsor Estate also purchased the current lease on the island, giving them complete control over its future development.

Even in 1880 Barry Island was still a long way from the ravages of the Industrial Revolution, and was popular for day visitors from Cardiff; in 1876 12,000 people used the ferry to experience a day out. Mixed bathing was not allowed, and Whitmore Bay was divided equally into two halves for males and females. Although hundreds of tourists visited the island for picnics and boating, by 1881 the population of Barry was still only 500 people.

Meanwhile, some 20 miles to the north and west of Barry Island, around the South Wales coalfield, the Industrial Revolution had been well under way for more than a century. In the west, in the lower Swansea, Neath and Afan valleys and around Llanelli, the world's greatest metallurgical smelting industry had developed since the end of the 16th century. Metallic ores of copper, zinc, tin, mercury and gold were being brought in by ship to

This photo mosaic of Barry Island was taken in 1884. The lone Marine Hotel and pier can be seen on the skyline to the far right of the island. *G. Beaudette Collection, National Museum of Wales*

Swansea Docks from North Wales, Cornwall, Ireland, Spain, Cuba and South America. Copper smelters were belching out thick, noxious, acidic smoke over the local hills, their smelters fed by coal from numerous small coal mines around the Swansea area.

In the north-east of the South Wales coalfield, local ironworks had developed, utilising the local resources of iron ore, limestone and coal. After the discovery by Abraham Darby in Ironbridge (1709) of how to smelt iron ore in a blast furnace using coal rather than charcoal, this iron-making technology transferred to the heads of the South Wales valleys. Industrial towns such as Blaenavon, Tredegar, Merthyr Tydfil and Aberdare were busy creating iron products for the developing Industrial Revolution all around the world. By 1850, 40% of Britain's total iron output was produced from Welsh Ironworks. Tramways and canals first connected these ironworks following the natural river drainage systems to docks built at the mouths of the rivers at Cardiff and Newport.

The first steam railway locomotive in the world was built in 1804 by Cornish inventor Richard Trevithick. It hauled a train along the tramway of the Penydarren ironworks, south of Merthyr Tydfil, comprising 10 tons of iron and 70 passengers in five wagons over 9 miles down the valley along the tramroad. Unfortunately these pioneering locomotives were thwarted by the brittle nature of the cast-iron rails, which easily cracked. In 1879 at Blaenavon, cousins and industrial chemists Percy Carlyle Gilchrist and Sidney Gilchrist Thomas discovered a way of removing unwanted phosphorous from the iron-making process, thus paving the way for the modern steel-making industry. Scottish-born American industrialist Andrew Carnegie invested in this steel-making patent; this sparked off the steel-making industry in North America, which in turn had a huge influence on the modern world.

By the late 19th century the early tramways and canals linking the industries, coal mines and ports were being replaced by the coming of railways to South Wales. The first railway to develop east-west links was the South Wales Railway, which had a plan to link Chepstow in the east, through Newport, Cardiff, Swansea, Llanelli and Carmarthen, to Fishguard on the West Wales coast. The line was completed between 1850 and 1863 to become today's South Wales main line. A railway network linking the iron town of Merthyr Tydfil and the ports of Cardiff and Penarth

was developed by the Taff Vale Railway between 1840 and 1862. The ironworks at the head of the eastern valleys at Tredegar were linked to the port at Cardiff by the Rhymney Railway in 1858. Such was the lucrative nature of the South Wales coalfield that many railway companies were created or moved in to construct lines to exploit the natural resources of the central and eastern South Wales valleys. These included the Llynvi & Ogmore Railway (1883), the Rhondda & Swansea Bay Railway (1882), the London & North Western Railway (1869), and the Brecon & Merthyr Railway (1859).

By 1884 the valleys of the Taff, Ebbw, Cynon, Sirhowy, Ogmore, Neath and Tawe were bustling with activity, with coal mines, industries and ports all linked by an ever-expanding network of railway lines.

The origins of Barry Docks and its associated railway lines can be traced back to a moment in time and place. The last area of South Wales to be heavily exploited for its

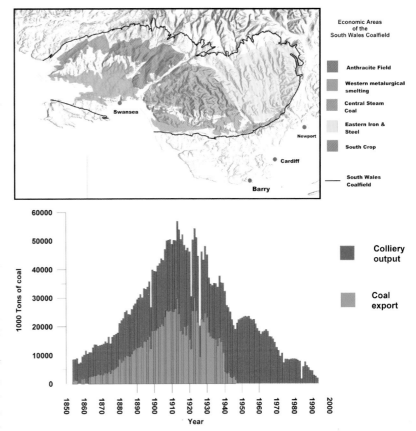

Economic Areas
of the
South Wales Coalfield

Anthracite Field

Western metalurgical smelting

Central Steam Coal

Eastern Iron & Steel

South Crop

South Wales Coalfield

Colliery output

Coal export

TOP The geo-economic divisions of the South Wales coalfield. *Peter Brabham/ Catherine Preston, Cardiff University*

ABOVE This graph shows the colliery output and export statistics for the whole of the South Wales coalfield, and the rapid rise and fall of coal-mining in the area. The peak of the coalfield trade was in 1912, when more than 50% of all coal mined was exported through the docks at Newport, Cardiff, Penarth, Barry, Neath, Swansea, Llanelli and Burry Port. Coal exportation died suddenly after the Second World War, mainly due to the change of global shipping from coal- to oil-fired boilers, together with competition from other countries.

of Llandinam sank the Maindy pit at Ton Pentre, Rhondda Fawr, to prove some of the richest coal seams in the world at that time. This 'Welsh steam coal' was perfect for fuelling the expanding number of steamships and navies around the world, so there was a great demand for export through Cardiff Docks. The consortium led by David Davies became the Ocean Coal Company, one of the major players in the coalfield. The sudden boom in coal mines and colliery output in the second half of the 19th century suddenly overwhelmed the exporting capabilities of the docks at Cardiff, then served by the Taff Vale and Rhymney Railways.

The building of Barry Docks

In the 1860-80 period, with the ever-increasing output of the coal mines of South Wales, there was an increasing demand for dock facilities in Cardiff. The original 1839 Bute Dock was expanded at a cost of half a million pounds with the construction of the Bute East Dock in 1859. To take some pressure off Cardiff, a small dock was also opened by a subsidiary company of the Taff Vale Railway in 1865 at Penarth at the mouth of the River Ely. However, the collieries owned by the Marquis of Bute had priority rights over the coal traffic from the Rhondda Valleys, and as a result coal trains owned by the Ocean Coal Co were taking nearly a day to cover the 25 miles between pit and port. In a decade from 1874 the coal export trade through Cardiff docks had expanded by 200%. David Davies of Llandinam, Chairman of the Ocean Coal Co, had previous experience of developing railways in Mid Wales, and his company put pressure on the Bute Trustees to further expand Cardiff Docks. This resulted in the construction of the Roath Dock in 1887 and finally the Queen Alexandra Dock in 1907.

ABOVE The construction of Barry No 1 dock with coal tips, just prior to being filled with water in June 1889. The dock is 3,400 feet long, 1,100 feet wide and has a maximum water depth of 37ft 9in. Each berth has high-level staithes, allowing individual coal trucks to deposit their contents into the ship's hold. *National Museum of Wales photo archive*

RIGHT The opening ceremony of Barry Docks: a group photograph taken at the lock gates. *National Museum of Wales photo archive*

steam coal was the interior of the central valleys, which included the valleys of the Rhondda Fawr and Fach. The first coal mine was developed in the upper reaches of the Rhondda Valleys in 1853, when the Marquis of Bute sunk a colliery at Treherbert to prove rich seams of quality coal in the central coalfield. This event triggered a new branch line off the main Taff Vale Railway at Pontypridd to access the upper reaches of the Rhondda, which was completed in 1855. In 1864 a consortium of investors led by David Davies

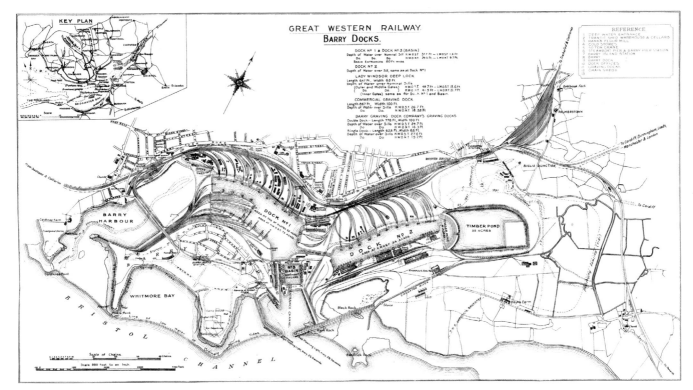

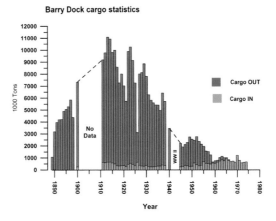

Barry Dock cargo statistics

A second option mooted by the disgruntled colliery owners was to develop a brand new dock on the South Wales coastline. In 1880 a consortium of Rhondda mine-owners led by David Davies and including Archibald Hood, Walter Insole, Crawshay Bailey and John Cory commissioned a feasibility study by H. M. Brunel, son of the great Isambard. A number of options were looked at, but the tidal estuary around Barry Island on land owned by Lord Windsor (outside the influence of the Marquis of Bute) was chosen as the most suitable location. Lord Windsor was keen to see his land and island being developed. The first Barry Dock bill in 1883 was defeated in the House of Lords, but a second bill was passed a year later by Parliament despite fierce opposition, and received the Royal Assent on 14 August 1884. The Act not only allowed the development of a dock over a 200-acre area, but also the construction of another 68 miles of associated railway lines to penetrate deep into the coalfield. Construction began just three months after the Act was passed. The contract for the main dock excavation was won by Thomas Walker of Westminster under the engineering supervision of (Sir) John Wolfe Barry, H. M. Brunel and T. Forster Brown of Cardiff.

Progress on the 75-acre dock project was dramatic and the excavation began with the cutting of the first sod by Lord Windsor on 14 November 1884. Three thousand construction workers (navvies) and 30 locomotives were used to excavate 5 million cubic yards of estuarine muds and clays. The curved design of the dock was dictated by the original shape of the tidal estuary between the mainland and Barry Island. More than 150 people were killed during the rapid construction of the docks, many buried in landslides caused by ground failures in the wet clay excavations. Water started to fill the newly constructed dock in June 1889 and an opening ceremony was planned for 18 July, five years after the Act of Parliament had been passed. David Davies led the opening ceremony, but died less than a year later.

No 1 Dock at Barry was the largest enclosed dock in the world. The cost of building the docks and railways was around £2 million, a phenomenal amount of money by today's standards. When the Act of Parliament was passed, the venture was called the Barry Dock & Railway Company, but this was changed in 1891 to the Barry Railway Company, listed on the Stock Exchange under railways rather than docks.

Barry Docks was designed entirely for the export of coal. The lock basin was 500 feet wide by 600 feet long, an area of about 7 acres. The total length of quayage around No 1 Dock was nearly 2 miles, encapsulating an area of 40 acres. There were 41 hydraulically powered hoists, with raised rail access embankments to the high-level tipping points at staithes spaced at different distances to suit different sizes of ships. Hydraulic power was supplied by two dock pump houses, one of which survives to this day.

Coal trucks were delivered by 'shunters', and were loaded individually by 'tippers' into the ship's hold, while 'trimmers' levelled the coal inside the hold by hand to ensure stability at sea. Great care was taken not to crush the coal, as large-lump coal was at a premium for steamships. The role of the

ABOVE An official Great Western Railway map of Barry Docks from 1923. At this time the Great Western Railway and the London & North Eastern Railway owned the largest dock systems in the world. *National Museum of Wales photo archive*

LEFT Incomplete export and import statistics for Barry Docks compiled from various sources. The rise in coal exports from the dock opening in 1898 to the peak of more than 11 million tons in 1913 was dramatic. The graph clearly reveals that Barry was essentially a coal-exporting port, with little cargo coming back in. The decline of coal exporting through the docks after the Second World War was not made up with other cargo types, and this had a massive impact on the docks and the town.

9

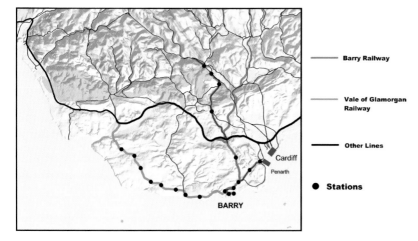

Barry Railway

Vale of Glamorgan Railway

Other Lines

● Stations

The associated Barry Railway

The 52 miles of running line built by the Barry Railway had one purpose only, to strike deep into the expanding coalfield to attract coal traffic to the docks. The system also had 17 stations, 51 signal boxes, two engine sheds and a repair works. To this extent the design was ruthless. The railway lines running north and eastward out of Barry had specific purposes:

■ A short easterly line running towards Penarth Docks to intercept the Taff Vale Railway at Cogan and Penarth Docks. The line was virtually level throughout, the only engineering feature of note being the 222-yard Cogan Tunnel. A through passenger service was developed between Barry and Cardiff Riverside station in 1893.

■ A northerly freight and passenger line engineered by (Sir) James W. Szlumper, which climbed over the limestone rim of the coalfield, then descended steeply towards Pontypridd through a 1,327-yard tunnel, ending at sidings at Trehafod in the Rhondda Valley. The economic purpose of this line was to tap into the vast coal-mining output of the expanding Rhondda Valleys coal mines. The line also required the excavation of a tunnel 1 mile 107 yards long through the hill at Wenvoe to avoid steep gradients. This line also had a short spur to connect with the GWR South Wales main line at St Fagans, and was completed by November 1888. The Barry Railway also built a large station at Pontypridd Graig and four intermediate stations (Wenvoe, Creigiau, Efail Isaf and Treforest) to accommodate passenger traffic, which commenced in March 1896.

■ A north-easterly freight-only line to tap into the eastern coalfield, which diverged from the Pontypridd line at Tyny-Caeau junction just north of St Fagans. However, the topography was against the construction of this line, as the Barry Railway had to cross over the Taff, Senghenydd and Rhymney valleys and their associated railways. This was achieved by breaching the southern rim of the coalfield through a tunnel, then crossing the Taff valley in the Taff Gorge by means of the 516-yard-long, 120-foot-high Walnut Tree lattice girder viaduct, opened in 1901. The Senghenydd and Rhymney valleys were crossed by two more large viaducts, Penyrheol Viaduct and the 50-foot-high Llanbradach Viaduct, built in 1905.

trimmer was crucial, as more than one coal ship capsized when the cargo moved in rough seas. Like coal miners, trimmers suffered from pneumoconiosis from constantly breathing in coal dust. Some 108 miles of railway sidings were constructed around the environs of the docks to accommodate the hundreds of weekly coal trains from the valleys. As a fully laden coal ship could only leave Barry Dock during a 2-hour window around high tide, ships' captains were always anxious to 'catch the tide' to avoid being laid up for 12 hours and losing money. Bribery between the ships' captains and the tippers and trimmers was commonplace to complete the loading before high tide.

The effect of the dock on the Welsh coal export trade was dramatic. One month after opening, 8,200 tons of coal was shipped out in one day, with a million tons of coal being exported by 600 ships in the first year of operation. So busy was the original No 1 Dock that a second 34-acre dock, No 2, was excavated to the east, under powers obtained by an 1893 Act of Parliament, and opened without ceremony in 1898. David Davies had died in 1890, and the chairmanship of the Barry Docks board passed to coal owner Archibald Hood. On construction, a geological fault was encountered, which meant that a cliffline had to be cut back further into Barry Island to provide solid foundations for cranes. This allowed the construction of a Mole promontory into No 1 Dock, thus further increasing the dock's capacity. Ships could leave Barry Docks in two ways, either via the 80-foot-wide gates of the No 3 Basin locks or at low tide by the 647-foot-long, 65-foot-wide Lady Windsor lock.

The building of Barry Docks had a massive influence on the village of Barry, whose population grew from 494 in 1881, to 13,278 in 1891, and 27,030 in 1901. A new bustling town of Barry suddenly grew around the docks, initially with temporary timber houses for the navvies. Within a decade housing syndicates had built a new town, with an infrastructure of schools, libraries and shops. By 1903, after an architectural competition, Barry had built a large Town Hall to show off its importance.

The zenith of trade in Barry Docks was achieved in 1913 when more than 11 million tons of coal was exported, 30% of the total trade of the South Wales ports. Imports were small by comparison; at the eastern end of No 2 Dock a timber pond was built for storing tree trunks imported from Scandinavia soaked in water for use underground as pit props in the coal mines.

It is worth noting that the Barry Railway never ran direct to a single coal mine in South Wales; it was built purely as a means of allowing coal trains originating on other railway lines in the South Wales coalfield direct and fast access to Barry Docks. The strategic nature of the Barry Railway lines can be seen in the accompanying map.

The railway west out of Barry along the coast was subject to a different Act of Parliament. The Vale of Glamorgan Railway construction commenced in 1894, resulting in 20¾ miles of double track to join the GWR main line at Coity. The purpose of this line was to tap into the coal mines of the southern part of the central coalfield around Bridgend, Maesteg and the Ogmore valleys, as well as running a passenger service. Although nominally independent of the Barry Railway, the VoG had no stock of its own, and traffic

This hand-coloured Barry Docks postcard dating from 1898 shows the wide variety of both sailing ships and steamships using the docks at this period.

Peter Brabham collection

was handled by the 148 available locomotives owned by the Barry Railway. The most notable construction on the VoG line is Porthkerry Viaduct to the west of Barry, flanked by two short tunnels; it is constructed of local limestone, with 16 arches and a rail deck 110 feet above the ground. The line was opened on 1 December 1897, only to close one month later when the easterly embankment to Porthkerry Viaduct, founded on clay rather than bedrock, failed, causing the first pillar and arch to move. It took more than two years to repair the viaduct, and in the meantime a temporary diversion around it was constructed. The completed VoG line reopened to freight and passenger traffic in January 1900.

The Barry Island branch line

As the town of Barry developed, locals and visitors flocked over to the former island's two beaches. To accommodate the tourists, it was originally planned to build a tram track from the Barry Railway station across to the island, but it was considered that this would not cope with the large number of summer visitors. In 1896 the Barry Company obtained an Act of Parliament to build a short three-quarter-mile-long branch line across to the former island. A new embankment had to be built across the old harbour with a road running alongside, with a steel girder bridge over the dock sidings.

The Barry Island branch line opened in 1896 and on its first day of operation, August Bank Holiday 1896, 30,000 visitors used the rail service. For the next 60 years hundreds of thousands of coal miners and their families came annually by train to Barry Island on Sundays and their rare Bank Holidays. Sunday excursion trains from the heads of the eastern valleys around Tredegar could access Barry Island direct over the normally freight-only Barry Railway lines; they would also come to Barry Island regularly from the English Midlands. In 1899 the branch line was further extended by driving a 280-yard tunnel through the central hill of the island to terminate at a pier station on the far

eastern shore, which opened on 27 June of that year. Bristol Channel steamers would dock at the pier and take holidaymakers on day trips over to Weston-super-Mare and Ilfracombe. The Barry Railway actually had its own fleet of four paddle steamers until 1910, when they were sold. Paddle steamers owned by P. & A. Campbell continued to use the Pier station until the late 1960s, and the pier rail service finally ended on 11 October 1971. There was also a short and rarely used siding that accessed the harbour breakwater via a short tunnel; this was only accessible by the lightweight Barry Railway 'F' class 0-6-0 tank engines.

The effect of building the embankment for the island branch line was to impound a lake between the embankment and the western extent of Barry Docks. This was called the 'West Pond', and this area would have an influence on the later part of the Barry scrapyard story.

The Great Western Railway era

The Barry Railway holds the distinction of being the first railway in the UK to use 0-8-0 tender locomotives; however, this was not by design, as it acquired two built by Sharp Stewart that were originally destined for Sweden, but the Swedish & Norwegian Railway Company could not pay for them. One famous train inaugurated in 1906 was the 'Ports to Ports Express', which ran between Barry and Newcastle-upon-Tyne, largely to accommodate the transfer of ships' crews between two of the UK's busiest ports.

In 1921, following the Railway Act, the Barry Railway was amalgamated with other railways into the Great Western Railway, which now owned the largest dock system in the world. At that time the Barry Railway owned 148 locomotives, a depot, railway workshops and a workforce of 3,000 people. The GWR largely replaced the Barry locomotive fleet with larger 2-8-0 tanks, and by 1930 most of the original Barry Railway locomotives had been scrapped or sold to industry. The Barry Railway 'B' and 'B1' class 0-6-2 tanks were re-boilered by the GWR and lasted until 1951. This post-war period coincided with the start of a general decline in coal export traffic in South Wales and the decline of the docks.

By January 1923 the Railway Act had taken effect and now, under the control of a single company, there was a great deal of track infrastructure duplication in the South Wales valleys. Just under 3 miles of the Rhymney branch of the Barry Railway became redundant. Two substantial Barry Railway steel lattice viaducts (Penyrheol and the larger Llanbradach), which crossed the Senghenydd and Rhymney valleys, were demolished in 1937; the 16-span, 90-foot-high Llanbradach Viaduct had only been built by the Barry Railway in 1904 at a cost of £250,000. The Barry Railway's depot at Hafod in the Rhondda closed in 1925, and the company's station at Pontypridd Graig closed in 1930, passenger traffic being diverted to the town's much larger Taff Vale Railway station.

The decline of Barry Docks and the railway

The zenith of the coal industry in South Wales was in 1913 when 230,000 miners, employed in 620 mines, produced 57 million tons of coal, of which 29.8 million tons (52%) was exported though the South Wales ports. Welsh steam coal was regarded as the perfect fuel for ocean-going steamships such as *Titanic* and the world's navies. Depots of Welsh steam coal were set up all over the world, fostering multi-cultural links between the Welsh port and the world that still has its legacy today, including a strong Greek and Italian community.

After the First World War the coal export trade became dislocated and this resulted in a period of economic depression in the 1930s. Foreign countries such as Poland introduced economic tariffs on Welsh coal to protect their own markets. At this time many ships were becoming oil-fired, reducing the global demand for steam coal. By the inter-war years coal exporting through Barry had dropped to half that of the 1913 peak.

During the Second World War Barry Docks saw an increase in coal traffic, exporting 13½ million tons between 1939 and 1945. The docks also suffered seven Luftwaffe bombing raids between July 1940 and July 1941, but by comparison to nearby Swansea and Cardiff the damage and death toll was minor. Later in the war, Barry Docks played a major role in the importing of railway locomotives from the USA; in 1944 more than 350 American locomotives were recorded hidden away on sidings belonging to the Barry Railway. Barry Docks was also chosen to store hydrocarbon products for the American war effort in France, and a huge storage depot was built at the south-eastern end of the docks. The railway sidings on the southern side of No 1 Dock and on the Mole were lifted and a tank farm constructed. Barry was a major storage depot for whale oil, which was used to make margarine, cooking oil and soap.

For the invasion of Europe in 1944, military vehicles and troop tents were camouflaged in Porthkerry Park, west of Barry. Twenty-one ships left Barry after the invasion, full of troops and equipment. Barry also handled armament imports for the Royal Navy armaments depot at Caerwent, which was transferred to US Army use in 1967 until its closure in 1993. US armament ships moored outside the docks in designated explosive anchorages in the Bristol Channel, and ammunition was ferried into the docks by smaller coasters to avoid the chance of a fully laden armament ship exploding inside the dock and causing catastrophic damage.

After the Second World War the railways were nationalised and the docks came under the ownership of the British Transport Commission. In the 1950s the West Pond was used as a landfill site; using a series of movable railway sidings, trainloads of industrial waste were tipped, gradually infilling the pond to reclaim new land from the lake. In December 1959 the locomotive repair works at Barry Docks was closed. The various tank farms that were built from the late 1950s onwards around the western end of Barry Docks contained a cocktail of chemicals including heavy fuel oil, coal tar, molasses, methanol, kerosene, sodium hydroxide, styrene, lubricating oil, sodium tetrachloride, phenol, benzene, isopropanol, methylated sprits, tri-ethylene glycol, diesel, jet fuel and cashew nut shell liquid, which accounted for the pungent aroma often encountered by any visitor to the docks during that period.

A problem that Barry Docks had following the war was the limited size of the dock gates, restricting access by the ever-increasing size of modern shipping. Large oil tankers destined for South Wales refineries were attracted to Milford Haven with its huge natural harbour. In 1962 the British Transport Docks Board was created as a Government-owned body to manage various ports formerly owned by the rail industry, including Barry. In 1965 a new dock at Portbury at the mouth of the River Avon just across the Bristol Channel was planned, which was another blow to the long-term prospects of Barry. The Portbury dock was finally constructed between 1972 and 1977.

The railway lines of the Barry Railway suffered greatly during the 1960s. Passenger services from Pontypridd to Barry ceased on 10 September 1962, and the 17-mile Rhondda branch from Cadoxton to Trehafod (Barry sidings) closed to all traffic on 30 March 1963; the northernmost part of the line from Treforest to Trehafod had closed earlier in 1956 due to subsidence problems in Pontypridd Graig Tunnel. The Rhymney branch also closed in March 1963, although part of the line from Penrhos from the east over Walnut Tree Viaduct remained open until 1967 to allow access to the Taffs Well dolomite works. Although scheduled for closure, the freight lines closed prematurely in 1963 due to the strategic signal box at Tyn-y-Caeau Junction being destroyed by fire. The last train ran over Walnut Tree Viaduct on 14 December 1967, and the impressive structure was demolished in September 1969; all but one of the remaining masonry piers had been taken down in 1973.

The short tunnel extension from Barry Island station to the Pier station was closed in July 1976 and is now used as a firing range. Apart from a final one-off rail tour in April 1973, the pier line had not been used since *Balmoral* last called at the Pier station in October 1971. The Vale of Glamorgan line lost its passenger service in 1965, but remains open to provide 'merry-go-round' coal train access to Aberthaw power station, and is also regularly used as a diversionary route for weekend engineering work on the South Wales main line. The passenger service on the Vale of Glamorgan line was reinstated in 2005, providing Bridgend to Cardiff

No. 2 Dock. Barry Docks.

A Barry Docks postcard dated 1924 shows far fewer sailing ships and more steamships using the docks by that time.

Peter Brabham collection

commuter trains and some limited access to the airport. The original Barry Railway link line from Cadoxton to Cogan is now the functioning Cardiff to Barry railway line, as the original Great Western line via Penarth was severed at Penarth station on 6 May 1968. In June 1969 the Barry Island branch line was reduced to single track, seriously reducing the capabilities of handling excursion traffic.

The major post-war industrial development at Barry Docks was the construction in 1952 of a plastics manufacturing complex by Distillers Limited at the far eastern end of No 2 Dock employing 600 people, one of the largest works of its type in Europe. This industry still exists today as the Dow Corning works, specialising in the manufacture of silicon-based fluids, gums and rubbers, and petrochemical tanker trains still visit the docks to service this factory. On 27 December 1997 one train of nine wagons containing Vinyl Chloride Monomer (VCM), a flammable liquefied gas, derailed at low speed on a hand-operated set of points in the docks and one wagon turned over. A thousand local people had to be evacuated from their homes while the flammable gas was pumped out of the overturned wagon.

The significant increase in the post-war import trade was through the Geest Line banana boats sailing between the West Indies and Barry, commencing in 1957. The dock also continued to handle fruit from Morocco and grain to the Rank flour mill. In 1962 a Government report on the state of UK ports recommended that Barry Docks be totally closed, although this was not acted upon. Ironically, during the 1970s and 1980s miners' strikes coal was actually imported into Barry Dock from the opencast mines of the USA, under much local protest.

In 1969 the Government's research council vessel base was transferred from Plymouth to Barry. In 1981 the British Transport Docks Board was privatised, becoming Associated British Ports. In the 1990s the NERC Government research vessel base was transferred away from Barry to a brand new facility at Southampton, and the Geest banana boats left Barry in 1993. In 2012 No 1 Dock is totally empty,

apart from the weekend of the annual waterside festival, with only the rare sight of a ship docking at No 2 Dock.

Over the last 20 years the mostly derelict Barry Docks has begun to be redeveloped. The sidings and coal tips on the north side of Nos 1 and 2 Docks have been levelled. A new docks access road has been constructed, with luxury housing, a supermarket, a hotel and associated out-of-town shopping. The contaminated topsoil has been skimmed off and sealed in the old graving dock. On the southern side of No 1 Dock the tank farms and NERC vessels base have been demolished and the site is totally barren. This derelict land in the south and at the West Pond site is now under active development for the 'Barry Waterside' housing redevelopment scheme, with a new access road to be built to Barry Island.

Barry Island – the day-trippers' destination

In the early 19th century thousands of people visited Barry Island by horse-drawn coaches from Cardiff for a summer day out on the island. After the construction of the docks this practice continued, and with the building of the island branch line people now came by train. One interesting aspect of Barry is the unusual close juxtaposition of major seaport and popular tourist beach resort. In 1909 the Earl of Plymouth gave the Barry Island foreshore and associated land to Barry Urban District Council; the tourist facilities on the island grew with the demand, and a new wide promenade was constructed. In the 1920s major developments such as the Cold Knap gardens and lake were constructed by Barry Council, and in 1924 the famous fairground was built on Barry Island. Such was the demand for excursion trains to the island that the station track layout had to be remodelled in 1929, with two new signal boxes and extra sidings to increase capacity. In the 1930s London Paddington to Barry Island excursion trains were regularly hauled by GWR 'Saint' class locomotives. In 1934 the Dudley Co-operative Society chartered ten ten-coach trains on the same day to Barry Island, which must have left Dudley almost empty! Charter trains would often leave the Bristol area at 6.00am, arriving at Barry Island by 8.00am. It was commonplace for Barry Island station to handle 30,000 passengers on a Bank Holiday Monday or a summer Sunday.

In the post-war era excursion trains from the valleys and the English Midlands were commonplace, especially on Bank Holiday weekends. Between 5.00pm and 8.00pm on a Sunday evening in 1957, as well as the scheduled valley trains, as many as nine long-distance excursion trains returned from Barry Island to destinations including Worcester, Brownhills, Swindon, Cheltenham and Shrewsbury. A wide variety of locomotive types could work to the island, including GWR 'Stars', 'Halls', 'Counties', 'Granges', 'Manors' and 'Castles', as well as BR Standard Classes 4 and 5; even a 'Britannia' 'Pacific' has been recorded at the island station. Favourites among photographers were the ex-LNWR 0-8-0 'Super D' locomotives on ten-coach excursions originating from towns at the head of the eastern valleys. Regular valley traffic was usually hauled by the 0-6-2 '56XX' tank engines, which could handle seven-coach trains back up the valley gradients; seven coaches was the length limit of most of the valley lines platforms. On Bank Holiday Monday in August 1957, 31 trains left Barry Island station between 5.00pm and 10.00pm.

In the 1960s the steam locomotives had been replaced by diesel multiple units (DMUs), which were known to sag so much under the weight of so many passengers getting on at Barry Island that the doors would not close properly. It was also not unusual to see 20 or more red double-decker buses coming in convoy down from the valleys chartered for chapel or pub outings.

Many people will associate Barry Island with the Butlins holiday camp, opened in June 1966, the last camp to be built by Butlins in the UK. Its construction was hotly opposed, as it was to be built on Nell's Point, a popular walking area for local people. Of the 800 wooden chalets, some had a lovely view of the docks with the oil tanks and scrapyard. By the 1970s, with the advent of the package holiday, people had turned away from many UK holiday destinations, while the opening of the Severn Bridge in September 1966 allowed much quicker access for car owners from South Wales to the West Country resorts. Barry Island, like many of the UK's once buoyant holiday resorts, saw a dramatic decline in tourism. Butlins sold its camp to Majestic Holidays in 1989 and, despite promises of major investment programmes, it soldiered on until final closure in 1996 after major storm damage. The site was sold to the Vale of Glamorgan Council, the derelict camp was razed to the ground and the land redeveloped to provide luxury housing built on the top of Nell's Point, again against local objections.

In 1997 the Vale of Glamorgan Council financially supported the opening of a VoG/Barry heritage railway, and a tourist line commenced operations in May 1998 using a £3 million finance package from the Welsh Assembly Government. The line was run by volunteers using small industrial tank engines relocated from the Butetown Historical Railway Society in Cardiff Bay. A short line running between the island station and the Barry Docks goods shed was created, and the line was later extended to Woodham Halt near Barry Town in 2004. Visiting steam engines (some which had been renovated from Woodham

Brothers' scrapyard at Barry) were seen once again working over the island branch line. Dramatically, in December 2007 the Council terminated its £65,000 annual grant to the Vale of Glamorgan Railway; a new lease was won under tender by Cambrian Transport, as its bid did not require continued financial support by the VoG Council. Under acrimonious circumstances the Vale of Glamorgan Railway Company and all its rolling stock were evicted and dispersed to other heritage lines. Since 2008 Cambrian Transport has run three annual events using a visiting steam engine, and more regular holiday services using a DMU.

The long-term reinstatement of a regular tourist steam railway at Barry Island is uncertain. In 2007-10 Barry obtained modern notoriety as the town featured in the hit TV comedy series *Gavin and Stacey*, which has boosted tourism to the island. In May 2012 Barry shed was used for the first time to stable two LMS 'Black Five' locomotives between runs over the Central Wales Line. This interesting development may point to a future for Barry shed in servicing main-line steam engines visiting Cardiff on charter trains.

The role of Woodham Brothers at Barry Docks

The Woodham family, Albert Woodham and his father, first arrived in Barry in the 1890s, employed on the construction of the Barry Railway. The family business was started by Albert in 1892, working as porters in Barry Docks and trading as Woodham & Sons. Albert had five sons who would go to sea as youngsters. In 1939, one son, Dai, was called up and spent seven years away from Barry winning a British Empire Medal for bravery serving in the Royal Artillery in Italy. On discharge from the Army, Dai took charge of the business and obtained a company licence to work as porters, mainly ferrying cargoes between ships in Barry and Cardiff Docks. The company also handled scrap and recyclable material from the ships that used the port; the latter included rope, whale oil and old firebars from the ships' boilers.

The company name was changed to Woodham Brothers Ltd around 1950, and by later in that decade Dai Woodham had developed the family business working with his brother Billy, who passed away in 1974. With the falling number of ships using the port, the Woodham business did what modern small businesses are told to do – diversify and look at new market opportunities. At that time British Railways was going through a major transformation. The number of freight wagons was being reduced by half a million and steam engines were being gradually displaced by diesels. Woodham Brothers had begun to cut up condemned railway wagons in 1957. Meanwhile the British Railways works could not cope with the vast numbers of steam engines they had to scrap, and a backlog was developing at major locations such as Swindon. To solve the problem, the decision was made to sell withdrawn steam locomotives to private scrapyards. Woodham Brothers saw a business opportunity, and would play a significant role in the railway scrapyard contracting business. In Dai Woodham's words, 'It was a wonderful gravy train and I had to get on it.' He spent a week in Swindon at meetings and watching how the works cut up steam locos to extract the various types of metal. By 1959 Woodham Brothers was ready to bid for steam engines from British Railways to scrap at Barry Docks, and the rest, as they say, is history.

ABOVE This aerial photograph of circa 1920 shows the entrance to Barry Docks, No 3 Basin and No 1 Dock. The two entrances for ships via a lock and a basin are clearly visible. Note the large number of coal tipping facilities and the paddle steamer docking at the Pier station (bottom left), which is accessed by a railway tunnel from Barry Island station. The ladies' teacher training college (1914) is prominent on the hill behind the dock, as is the town gasworks, now the site of the Vale of Glamorgan Council Offices. *Air photo unit, Welsh Assembly Government*

ABOVE Barry Docks at its zenith: this *circa* 1907 photograph shows the remarkable number of coal trucks that were dealt with every day at the height of the coal trade. Trucks from the Rhondda collieries owned by Cory Brothers, Powell Dyffryn and Cambrian are all visible. Half a century later, these sidings will be the site of the Woodham's steam locomotive scrapyard. *Reflective Images of Wales*

ABOVE Barry Pier station is seen in an undated postcard from the early 1900s. Passengers would alight here to catch the Bristol Channel paddle steamers across to Somerset and North Devon.

ABOVE This aerial photograph of Barry Docks is looking eastward over No 1 Dock and the Mole promontory in 1932. The coal export trade has started to decline by this period but most of the coal-exporting infrastructure still remains intact. The railway tunnel portal on the island, allowing trains to access the Pier station, is visible on the extreme right. In the left foreground is the West Pond. *Royal Commission for Ancient Monuments in Wales*

LEFT GWR 'Star' class No 4018 *Knight of the Grand Cross* brings an excursion from the Midlands across Barry causeway to the Island station in the summer of 1935. Excited children are waving out of the windows. No 4018 was built at Swindon Works in April 1908 and remained in service until withdrawn from Stafford Road shed, Wolverhampton, in April 1951. Unfortunately the locomotive was scrapped eight years before GWR locomotives were being purchased for the scrapyard in Barry. *National Museum of Wales photo archive*

This aerial photograph of No 1 Dock at Barry is dated 20 September 1943. A white barrage balloon is visible on the Mole promontory, and the hydrocarbon tanks have an interesting 'road' camouflage pattern painted on their roofs. Interestingly these tanks do not appear on historical Ordnance Survey mapping of the same period for purposes of national security. *National Museum of Wales photo archive*

Another image taken on 20 September 1943. Note that the West Pond is totally intact, but does not seem to have any purpose linked to the docks. New tanks to store whale oil are being constructed on the Mole. *National Museum of Wales photo archive*

A USA 'S160' class 2-8-0 locomotive is being unloaded in the rain at Barry Docks in 1944. In that year author Eric Mountford counted more than 119 of these locomotives stored on the Barry Railway at Treforest, 152 at Penrhos and 84 in sidings at Cadoxton. Subsequently they would be shipped off to Europe and North Africa for the war effort. *National Museum of Wales photo archive*

17831

ABOVE This higher-altitude aerial image is dated 20 September 1943, and is looking westward over the old harbour and along the coastline towards Rhoose. The Vale of Glamorgan line's Porthkerry Viaduct is just visible on the western outskirts of Barry. *National Museum of Wales photo archive*

LEFT In this aerial image dated 24 May 1951, looking over Friar's Point, the West Pond area is now starting to be landfilled by progressive tipping from temporary sidings. The construction of more whale oil tanks on the Mole is progressing. *Air Photo Unit, Welsh Assembly Government*

By 7 August 1959, the whale oil tank farm on the Mole is now complete and the West Pond area is now totally infilled. Thousands of holidaymakers are enjoying the beach and the fairground in Whitmore Bay. The mile-long scenic railway was first built by Billy Butlin for the 1938 Glasgow Empire Exhibition, then dismantled and reconstructed at Barry. *Air Photo Unit, Welsh Assembly Government*

This crisp but undated air image is from the Tempest collection held by the National Museum of Wales. Six DMUs are in the sidings at Barry Island station, but no steam engines have yet accumulated in the docks. This would date the image to around 1959/60. *National Museum of Wales photo archive*

A second 1959/60 air image in the Tempest collection looks north over Barry Island and Nell's Point just before the building of Butlins holiday camp in 1965. *National Museum of Wales photo archive*

TOP GWR 0-6-2 tank No 357 heads the 1.50pm local to Barry out of Bridgend station over the Vale of Glamorgan line on 13 April 1954. The loco was originally built by North British in Glasgow for the Taff Vale Railway as No 124 in August 1915; it was rebuilt by the Great Western with a new boiler in 1924 and was withdrawn from traffic in January 1956. *John Wiltshire*

ABOVE GWR No 361 hauls the 1.50pm local train to Barry out of Bridgend station on 25 October 1954. The locomotive was originally built by Vulcan Foundry in July 1916 as Cameron Taff Vale Class A No 127. The locomotive was rebuilt with a GWR boiler in 1924 and renumbered 361; it was withdrawn in January 1957. Sadly, none of these GWR rebuilds of pre-Grouping locomotives survive in preservation as all were withdrawn a few years before Woodham Brothers purchased withdrawn BR locomotives. *John Wiltshire*

RIGHT Former LNWR 'G2A' class 'Super D' No 49174, based at Tredegar shed, powers a Barry Island excursion from Nantybwch (near Tredegar) over Barry Railway tracks at Tyn-y-Caeau Junction at 11.45am on Sunday morning, 10 July 1955. 'Super D' locomotives were normally used on coal and steel freights over the former LMS lines in the Eastern Coalfield, but at weekends they were often drafted in to haul long excursion trains to Barry Island over the freight line. Unfortunately no 'Super D' made it to Woodham Brothers' scrapyard; however, one example, BR No 49395, was preserved for the National Collection. After many years standing in the open air as a static exhibit at Ironbridge, No 49395 was restored to steam with the substantial financial backing of Pete Waterman, who in his youth worked as a fireman on these engines based around Birmingham.
John Wiltshire

Returning home from a day out at Barry Island at 7.22pm on Sunday 10 July 1955 is No 5698, hauling an Aberdare-bound excursion at Tyn-y-Caeau Junction on former Barry Railway lines. The Barry-Treforest freight line closed when the signalbox in the background was destroyed by fire in March 1963, which brought forward the closure decision.
John Wiltshire

Returning from a day out at Barry Island at 8.10pm on Sunday 10 July 1955, another 'Super D', No 49064, hauls a homeward-bound excursion at Tyn-y-Caeau Junction. The 'Super Ds' were too large to turn on the small turntable at Barry shed and were turned for the return journey by making a long circuit around Barry Docks. *John Wiltshire*

TOP Heading another homeward-bound excursion from Barry Island on the same day, 'Large Prairie' No 5195 hauls a 10-coach Treherbert-bound excursion in the setting sun at Tyn-y-Caeau Junction. At its peak 90 southbound loaded coal trains per day were booked to run to the docks; the trackbed now partly forms the route of the link road from the M4 to Cardiff Bay, and little evidence remains of the junction. *John Wiltshire*

ABOVE *Kyle of Lochalsh*, built in 1952 on the Tyne as the *Beverleygate*, received her new name in 1958 for Monroe Bros of Liverpool. She was used to carry coal from Barry to Irlam (Manchester Ship Canal) and also from Swansea to Bordeaux and Cork. She was eventually broken up in Greece in 1982. In the rear is *Kraljevica*, a Yugoslavian steam cargo-ship built in 1944 by Harland & Wolff on the Clyde as the *Empire Nerissa* for the Ministry of War Transport to a standard wartime design. She became the *Kraljevica* in 1959 for her new Yugoslav owners, and was scrapped in Yugoslavia in 1966. Both ships are seen on 9 July 1963 loading coal during the dying days of the coal export trade from Barry Docks. *John Wiltshire*

ABOVE This is the western end of Barry motive power depot and the Barry Island branch line on 30 July 1963. On shed can be seen a single GWR '72XX' 2-8-2T, plus 0-6-2T and 0-6-0 pannier tanks. Forty-eight years later a GWR 0-6-2 tank could still be found at the same location. *John Wiltshire*

LEFT GWR 0-6-2T No 6655 is seen hauling excursion stock into Barry station on 30 July 1963 while a group of ladies wait for the train back up the valleys. No 6655 was cut up in May 1965 in Llanelli. *John Wiltshire*

GWR 'Small Prairie' No 5574 has just brought a Stephenson Locomotive Society special into Barry Pier station on 13 July 1957 and is ready to return down the branch. The special toured over the Llantrisant-Cowbridge branch and down to Cardiff Riverside during the day out for the railway enthusiasts. No 5574 would find its way to Barry scrapyard in May 1962, and would be cut up in March 1965. *John Wiltshire*

These two views show the demolition of the Barry Railway's Walnut Tree Viaduct in the Taff Gorge on 28 September 1969. The viaduct was the means by which the Barry Railway crossed over the River Taff, the Taff Vale Railway, the Cardiff Railway and the Glamorganshire Canal in the narrow Taff Gorge to access the eastern valleys coalfield in the Rhymney Valley. The bridge was built in 1901 of steel lattice girders on seven masonry pillars 120 feet above the valley floor. Behind the bridge is the dolomite works associated with the Taffs Well limestone quarry. No regular passenger trains ran over the bridge, only specials to Barry Island. The last train crossed it on 14 December 1967. Little now remains of the viaduct or the dolomite works except one pillar commemorating the Queen's Silver Jubilee. Like the famous Crumlin Viaduct, little heed was taken in the 1960s of the industrial heritage significance of these structures in South Wales. *Both John Wiltshire*

This 1966 aerial photograph shows the western end of No 1 Dock at Barry, the West Pond site, the railway depot, the Barry Railway works and the island. The West Pond is now totally landfilled and three sidings have been laid on the area. It is obviously the summer – note the large number of people from the newly built Butlins holiday camp on Nell's Point swimming in the sea. Steam locomotives are accumulating on the redundant coal sidings. Virtually all the coal tips have been demolished by now, to be replaced by tank farms. *Air Photo Unit, Welsh Assembly Government*

This photo mosaic of three air images taken in July 1971 starts to show the dereliction of the western end of the docks. The Barry Railway locomotive works has now been demolished, and lines of steam locomotives are present in many of the sidings.
Cardiff University, School of Earth & Ocean Sciences photo archive

A crystal-clear Ordnance Survey air photograph of the whole extent of Barry Docks and the island, dated 1979. The large holiday complex of Butlins is clearly apparent on Nell's Point headland, and the UK Government's research vessel base has been built on the south side of **No 1 Dock.** *Reproduced by permission of Ordnance Survey on behalf of HMSO © Crown Copyright 2011. All rights reserved. Ordnance Survey licence number 100020212*

Echoes of the past: tall ship *Stavros S. Niarchos,* owned by the Tall Ships Youth Trust, enters Barry Dock in September 2004. The ship was only four years old when this photograph was taken. *Peter Brabham*

BELOW Echoes of the past: although the last Bristol Channel paddle steamers were scrapped in the 1960s, every summer the world's last ocean-going paddle steamer *Waverley* visits the Bristol Channel to re-create the great days out of 100 years ago, as seen here passing Flat Holm island in June 2011. *Peter Brabham*

BELOW Another photograph taken from Barry Island, looking north over the Main Yard, taken from an undated original slide by the late Hedley Davies. In the far background by the goods shed can be seen a line of three diesel locomotives, including Class 15 No D8026, which dates the image to the autumn of 1969. This was the peak of locomotive acquisitions, with more than 200 locomotives in the scrapyard. The oil tanker has Cory Brothers written on its side, a company that goes right back to the building of Barry Docks. *Hedley Davies*

This panoramic view, taken from Barry Island looking north over the western end of Barry Docks on 1 June 1967, illustrates the Main Yard and the West Pond sites. At this time there were just under 200 withdrawn steam locomotives scattered around the docks at a number of locations, and more were still arriving – the last batch arrived in September 1968. A large number of BR guard's vans have also arrived for cutting up, reflecting the downturn in freight traffic over the national network. Even more withdrawn steam engines are just visible in the Top Yard behind the chimney of the dock pump house. The hydrocarbon tanks in the right foreground are still active, as can be seen by the two lines of oil tankers in the sidings. *Peter Brabham collection*

2 Barry scrapyard locomotives in service and the decline of steam in the early 1960s

The story described in the rest of this book really begins on 1 December 1954, when British Railways unveiled its report *Modernisation and Re-equipment of British Railways*. One aspect was to phase out steam locomotives, to be replaced by diesel and electric traction. At the same time British Railways was still constructing its Standard locomotives. The last steam locomotive to be built, 9F No 92200 *Evening Star*, would be completed at Swindon Works in March 1960. In 1962 the Transport Act stipulated that the railways were to be economic and compete in a free market. This was an open door for the Chairman of British Railways, Richard Beeching, to instigate wholesale closure of many uneconomic railway lines. His report in 1963, *The Reshaping of British Railways*, was his master plan.

On nationalisation, Barry locomotive shed had an allocation of 84 GWR locomotives: 21 0-6-0 tank engines, 62 0-6-2 tanks, some of which were Great Western rebuilds of earlier locomotives, and one 2-6-2 'Prairie' tank. In 1953 it received a fleet of ten new BR Standard 3MT 2-6-2T '82XXX' class locomotives, but they proved to be not as powerful as the older GWR 0-6-2T '66XXs' and 2-6-2T '41XXs' and were limited to hauling six coaches up the valleys.

By early 1958 Derby-built diesel multiple units had arrived in South Wales, and within a year, after a short period of crew training, they had replaced steam-hauled passenger traffic on the valley lines. In 1963 English Electric Type 3 locomotives (later better known as Class 37) were introduced to haul the South Wales valleys coal traffic, and had a dramatic effect on the withdrawal of the steam tank engines in South Wales. Indeed, the Class 37s would continue to be the stalwarts of the South Wales freight trains for the next three decades. Barry steam depot was closed in September 1964 and converted into a wagon repair shed. It is reported that the last regular steam working on the old Taff Vale system was by 0-6-2T No 5692 working out of Radyr shed on 17 July 1965. In the latter half of the 1960s, the last bastions of steam would soldier on in the North West of England until August 1968.

This chapter features a selection of photographs mainly taken by John Wiltshire, who at that time lived on the outskirts of Cardiff. John worked as a Glamorgan Council architectural surveyor, which meant that he travelled all over South Wales during this period. He carried a camera with him at all times and managed to capture the end of steam on South Wales. He also paid photographic visits to the West Country to capture the end of the Somerset & Dorset line. The use of steam locomotives for regular freight and passenger services on South Wales' BR lines came to an end by 1965.

Most of the locomotives featured in this chapter will by chance on withdrawal be sold to Woodham's scrapyard in Barry Docks. Some unfortunately will be cut up, while others will survive to this day to haul tourists on heritage lines or on main-line charter trains.

GWR 2-8-0 No 3814 heads a westbound freight through Newport station on 27 July 1963. *John Wiltshire*

ABOVE GWR 2-8-0 No 3850 stands at a snowy Cardiff Canton depot on 4 March 1962. This depot closed to steam on 9 September 1962, and was demolished and replaced by a diesel depot. *John Wiltshire*

BELOW GWR 2-8-0 No 3802 is on the turntable at Cardiff Canton depot on 6 October 1962. *John Wiltshire*

ABOVE GWR pannier tank No 9488 is seen at Quakers Yard High Level station on 16 May 1964. No 9488 was withdrawn in April 1965 and was one of 20 '94XX' class locomotives to be sent for scrap at Barry Docks. Of those 20, only one, No 9466, survived being cut up and was returned to steam.

John Wiltshire

RIGHT GWR 2-8-0 No 3862 stands between No 6966 *Witchingham Hall* and BR '9F' No 92215 on shed at Cardiff Canton depot on 15 July 1962.

John Wiltshire

LEFT GWR 2-8-0 No 3814 was photographed at Bedminster, Bristol, on 19 October 1963. *John Wiltshire*

BELOW GWR 'Prairie' tank No 5553 is under overhaul at Caerphilly Works on 2 June 1961. *John Wiltshire*

GWR 'Large Prairie' No 4160 passes Cardiff Canton on a westbound passenger train in April 1962. *John Wiltshire*

TOP GWR 0-6-2T No 6696, seen at Rhoose station on the Vale of Glamorgan line on 2 June 1962, was withdrawn in December 1963 and sold to Woodham Brothers' scrapyard. It was one of the 84 locomotives that did not survive the scrapyard, being cut up by April 1964. *John Wiltshire*

ABOVE GWR 0-6-2 tank No 5688 passes St Athan RAF airfield on the Vale of Glamorgan line with a freight towards Barry on 14 October 1963. *John Wiltshire*

TOP GWR 2-8-0 tank No 4283 is westbound at Newport on 30 March 1963. It was withdrawn in October 1964 and cut up by Woodham Brothers in the spring of **1965.** *John Wiltshire*

ABOVE GWR No 7927 *Willington Hall* heads a westbound passenger train to Cardiff on the South Wales main line at Marshfield on 5 October 1963. *John Wiltshire*

GWR 'Large Prairie' No 6115 is shunting empty stock at Pontypool Road station on 22 August 1962. It was withdrawn from Severn Tunnel Junction shed in November 1964 and cut up at Woodham Brothers by the spring of 1965. *John Wiltshire*

GWR No 7819 *Hinton Manor* is seen at Oswestry MPD on 14 June 1956. *John Wiltshire*

GWR 0-6-2 tank No 5668 passes St Brides on 8 June 1963, with Newport Transporter Bridge in the background. *John Wiltshire*

GWR No 7820 *Dinmore Manor* waits for signals at Gloucester Central on 25 June 1964. *John Wiltshire*

No 6990 *Witherslack Hall* hauls an eastbound passenger train out of Newport Tunnels into the station on 20 July 1963. The locomotive was withdrawn from traffic in December 1965 and arrived at Woodham's scrapyard two months later.
John Wiltshire

GWR 0-6-2 tank No 5619 is seen at St Fagans on 2 March 1965. *John Wiltshire*

Also seen at the same spot on 2 March 1965 is GWR 2-8-2 tank No 7229.
John Wiltshire

GWR 'Castle' class No 5043 *Earl of Mount Edgcumbe* heads east out of Cardiff at Pengam Junction with the 10.30am Cardiff-Portsmouth train on 8 June 1963. *John Wiltshire*

Earl of Mount Edgcumbe passes through Newport station with a westbound parcels train for Cardiff on 22 September 1962, making three young trainspotters very happy. *John Wiltshire*

GWR 'Castle' No 5051 *Earl Bathurst* runs light engine through Neath General station on 17 October 1962. The locomotive was withdrawn from traffic in May 1963. *John Wiltshire*

GWR 'King' class No 6023 *King Edward II* is on shed at Cardiff Canton depot on 18 February 1962. No 6023 was withdrawn in June of that year and by a series of fortunate coincidences arrived at Barry scrapyard in December. *John Wiltshire*

TOP BR Southern Region 'West Country' Pacific No 34101 *Hartland* gets the right of way from Waterloo station, London, in March 1965. *Hartland* was withdrawn from traffic in October 1966 and was one of 18 locomotives of this class to end up in Barry scrapyard. *John Wiltshire*

ABOVE 'Merchant Navy' class No 35006 *Peninsular and Oriental S. N. Co*, passes Templecombe station running westbound towards Exeter on 1 September 1962. No 35006 was withdrawn from traffic in August 1964. Ten locomotives of this class ended up in Barry scrapyard. *John Wiltshire*

Unrebuilt 'West Country' No 34092 *City of Wells* wears full 'Golden Arrow' regalia at Stewarts Lane depot, London, *circa* 1957.
Peter Brabham collection

'West Country' No 34105 *Swanage* enters Templecombe station on 18 September 1959. *John Wiltshire*

LMS 0-6-0 No 44422 is seen at Cole station on the Somerset & Dorset line in April 1964. No 44422 was withdrawn from traffic in June 1965 and, together with two other locomotives of this class, ended up in Barry scrapyard.
John Wiltshire

ABOVE Somerset & Dorset '7F' 2-8-0 No 53808 shunts at Templecombe station on 11 September 1960. The locomotive was withdrawn in February 1964 and arrived in Barry scrapyard in June of that year with classmate No 53809. *John Wiltshire*

LEFT Somerset & Dorset '7F' 2-8-0 No 53809 is seen on shed at Bath MPD in April 1964. The locomotive was withdrawn in June 1964 and arrived in Barry scrapyard in August of that year. *John Wiltshire*

TOP A very grimy LMS No 45690 *Leander* enters Gloucester Eastgate station on 8 September 1962. *Leander* was withdrawn from traffic in March 1964 and ended up in Barry scrapyard with classmate *Galatea*. *John Wiltshire*

ABOVE LMS No 43924 passes Berkeley Road station, Gloucestershire, in the pouring rain on 23 May 1958. *John Wiltshire*

TOP The Somerset & Dorset Railway was truly one of the greatest places to be as a railway photographer in the early 1960s. A passenger train hauled by Fowler 7F No. 53809 and BR Class 5MT No. 73049 calls at Evercreech Junction on 1 September 1962. Note the two wonderful old ladies, one in the fur coat and the other walking a small dog, plus the railway photographer eating his sandwich at the far end of the platform. This image looks just like a scene out of an Agatha Christie novel! Fortunately locomotive No 53809 ended up in Barry scrapyard; unfortunately No 73049 was scrapped in June 1965 at Bird's scrapyard, Risca, **South Wales.** *John Wiltshire*

ABOVE The idyllic Welsh Borderlands with three steam trains in at the rural Three Cocks station near Hay on Wye, with 46512 leaving with a train to Brecon on the 7th June 1962. The line closed on the 31st December 1962 and the site is now a council depot. *John Wiltshire*

THIS PAGE TOP The only LNER locomotive to be sent for scrap at Barry scrapyard was 'B1' class 4-6-0 No 61264. The reason for this was that after it was withdrawn from traffic in 1965, it was used together with 16 other 'B1' locomotives as a Departmental Locomotive (No 29) and used as a boiler for heating carriages until September 1968. That is the excuse to include this crisp Kodachrome image of classmate 'B1' locomotive Departmental No 17 (BR No 60159), which is seen at Ipswich in April 1965 in use as a carriage heating boiler; it was scrapped in 1966. *John Wiltshire*

THIS PAGE CENTRE BR Standard tank No 80072 is seen near Pontardulais with the 4.00pm service to Swansea Victoria on 31 May 1963. *John Wiltshire*

THIS PAGE BOTTOM BR Standard tank No 80097 stands at Swansea Bay station on 24 July 1962. *John Wiltshire*

FACING PAGE TOP No 80097 is seen again, running westward from the LMS Swansea Victoria station, alongside Swansea Bay, in May 1963. On the other side of the hoardings was the trackbed of the famous Mumbles Railway, which closed on 5 January 1960, in hindsight a staggering display of industrial heritage vandalism. *John Wiltshire*

FACING PAGE BOTTOM BR Standard 9F 2-10-0 No 92245 hauls a Bradford to Bournemouth train through Midford station on the Somerset & Dorset line on 25 August 1962. As a railway photographer, if you could loop time, as in the film *Groundhog Day,* this might be a good place and time to do it! *John Wiltshire*

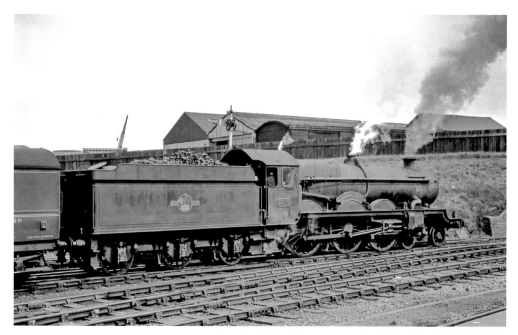

It would have been serendipitous if GWR No 7012 *Barry Castle* had ended up in Woodham's Barry scrapyard, but unfortunately it was cut up at Cashmore's scrapyard, Great Bridge, in February 1965. Here the locomotive is seen at Wolverhampton Low Level on an unknown date. However, the *Barry Castle* nameplates did make it to Barry as they were owned by Dai Woodham and were proudly displayed on his office wall. Sadly, one of the nameplates was stolen in a burglary at his old office in Thomson Street, Barry, and he was approached by persons unknown to buy it back on three occasions, but he just told the sellers why should he buy back something that he already owned? Dai Woodham sold the remaining *Barry Castle* plate at auction in 1994 just before he died.
Peter Brabham collection

It is 17 May 1963 at Radyr station and marshalling yards north of Cardiff, and the end of steam in the South Wales valleys is imminent. Brand new diesel D6839 (later Class 37) has just been delivered for service, while the fireman of GWR 0-6-2T No 6635 stops for a chat. D6839 was released into traffic on 3 May 1963, so is just two weeks old in this shot. No 6635 was withdrawn from service at Radyr shed in July 1964. The Class 37 diesels would go on to dominate South Wales freight traffic for more than three decades. *John Wiltshire*

The regular use of steam locomotives on the passenger services of the South Wales valley lines was displaced rapidly from 1958 by the introduction of the diesel multiple-units. Here a Derby Works DMU built in 1957 is seen at Llandow Halt on the Vale of Glamorgan line in May 1964. Passenger services on the VoG line ceased in June 1964, although they were restored in June 2005.
John Wiltshire

TOP On the South Wales main line in the early 1960s the passenger trains that were once the domain of the GWR 'King', 'Castle' and 'Hall' classes were being displaced by the diesel-hydraulic 'Westerns' and 'Hymeks', although 'Warships' were quite rare in South Wales at that time. 'Hymek' No D7023, introduced into service in 1961, leaves Newport station with the 9.20am London train on 9 April 1962. *John Wiltshire*

ABOVE The last main-line steam locomotive built at Swindon Works by British Railways, in March 1960, was '9F' freight locomotive No 92220 *Evening Star*, seen here on shed at Cardiff Canton depot on 30 May 1962. At this time the '9F' was based here, but would move in June 1962 to Bath Green Park for its photographically well documented passenger work on the Somerset & Dorset Railway. The loco is still extant, but did not go to Woodham Brothers' scrapyard as it was preserved directly for the National Collection from Cardiff East Dock shed in March 1965, after only five years of active work. *John Wiltshire*

The steam locomotive scrapyards of South Wales

Number of steam locomotives on British Railways

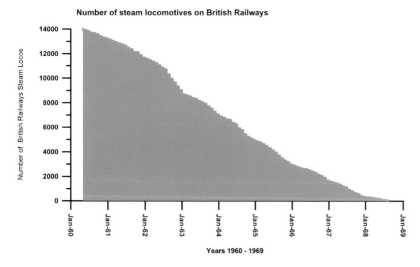

In December 1958 there were 16,108 steam locomotives working on British Railways, and this had dropped to 14,000 at the start of 1960. The last steam locomotive was withdrawn by British Railways on 1 August 1968. The accompanying graph shows the constant decline in working British Railways locomotives throughout the 1960s. Until 1959, all withdrawn locomotives were cut up in British Railway works, but on 25 March of that year the first locos were sold to private scrapyards. The first to accept them was Woodham Brothers of Barry Docks; these were GWR 2-6-0 'Moguls' Nos 5312, 5360, 5392 and 5397.

During the 1960s many more private scrapyards throughout the UK purchased steam locomotives from British Railways – more than 100 locations have been recorded. These yards ranged greatly in size from Grade 1 yards, which scrapped many hundreds of locomotives, to Grade 2 yards where 100 or so locomotives were scrapped, and Grade 3 and 4 yards, where the number was only in double or single figures. South Wales played a major part in locomotive scrapping, mainly due to the recycling of metal into the local steelworks or by export to other countries from the docks. The major sites in South Wales were as follows:

- Cashmore's was the major locomotive scrapping company in the UK, and had a number of UK sites. Its site in Newport Docks was a major player, scrapping more than 800 locomotives. Of particular interest is the fact that Cashmore's scrapped four GWR 'King' class locos, 37 'Castle' class and 43 Bulleid 'Pacifics'. The yard also scrapped GWR 'County' and 'Grange' locomotives, BR 'Britannias', 'WDs' and 82XXX and 84XXX classes that were not found at Barry scrapyard.
- Also in Newport Docks was J. Buttigieg, which scrapped more than 100 locomotives between 1960 and 1966, including 24 Bulleid 'Pacifics'.
- Bird's had four South Wales sites that between them scrapped more than 400 locomotives. The company's site at Risca disposed of GWR 'King' No 6028 and the Morriston site cut up eight 'Castle' class locomotives. The company disposed of 18 Bulleid 'light Pacifics' in South Wales.
- Hayes at Bridgend scrapped more than 300 locomotives, mostly from South Wales.
- G. Cohen had a site at Morriston, Swansea, that scrapped 172 locomotives.

The accompanying map shows the location of South Wales locomotive scrapyard sites, which in total scrapped more than 2,100 locomotives.

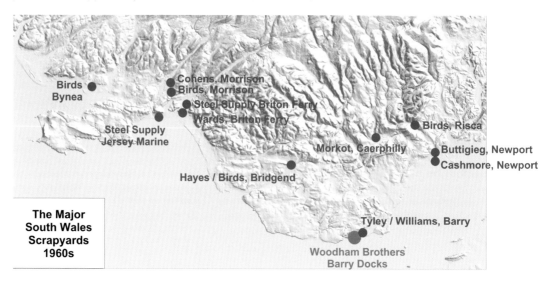

The Major South Wales Scrapyards 1960s

There is an ongoing debate about the accuracy of published records regarding the scrapping of British Railways locomotives. The following list is an approximate guide to the number of steam locomotives scrapped in the South Wales scrapyards:

Cashmore's	Newport	834
Hayes/Bird's	Bridgend	346
Bird's	Risca	204
Cohen's	Morriston	172
Ward's	Briton Ferry	159
Bird's	Morriston	154
Buttigieg's	Newport	107
Woodham Brothers	Barry Docks	84
Bird's	Bynea	55
Steel Supply	Jersey Marine	22

The other South Wales scrapyard sites were minor by comparison, scrapping 11 or fewer locomotives each.

The legacy of Woodham's Barry scrapyard is that, in not cutting up all its locomotives, they subsequently became available to be purchased for preservation. Thus,

locomotives of the former Great Western, London Midland & Scottish and Southern Railways have been preserved, together with British Railways Standard locomotives. Only one locomotive of the former London & North Eastern Railway found its way to Barry, the reason for this being rather straightforward. Magnificent LNER locomotives of the 'A1', 'A2', 'A3' and 'A4' classes were cut up by scrapyards in the east and north of the country supplying scrap steel for the blast furnaces of Glasgow, Motherwell, Consett, Middlesbrough, Corby and Sheffield. Thankfully, in the 1960s a few far-sighted individuals managed to purchase LNER locomotives at the end of their BR working lives. Significant locomotives such as *Blue Peter*, *Sir Nigel Gresley*, *Union of South Africa*, *Bittern*, 'B12' No 61572 and *Flying Scotsman* all live on. Thanks to the North Eastern Locomotive Preservation Group based on the North Yorkshire Moors Railway, a number of less glamorous LNER freight locos are still part of our historical record.

During the 1960s John Wiltshire travelled around Glamorgan and Monmouthshire and managed to document this dramatic period in the sudden demise of steam on beautiful Kodachrome film.

Railway locomotive preservationists look away now. This is the amazing sight on 24 February 1968 at Cashmore's, Newport, Monmouthshire, as rebuilt Bulleid 'West Country' No 34021 *Dartmoor* awaits its fate. You can play 'recognise the locomotive parts' with the huge scrap pile behind the locomotive. Cashmore's scrapped a staggering 834 standard gauge British Railways locomotives. Imagine present-day railway preservationists being able to collect spare parts from that scrap pile! *John Wiltshire*

FACING PAGE TOP The speed at which locomotives were cut up at Cashmore's is apparent here on 9 July 1967. *John Wiltshire*

FACING PAGE BOTTOM In this line-up of Bulleid Pacifics in Newport Docks awaiting scrapping on 10 February 1968, the photographers noted these as Nos 34108 *Wincanton*, 34104 *Bere Alston*, 34047 *Callington* and 34008 *Padstow*. *John Wiltshire*

THIS PAGE TOP Unrebuilt 'West Country' Pacific No 34066 *Spitfire* languishes in Buttigieg's yard at Newport on 31 December 1966. No 34066 was withdrawn from Salisbury in August 1966; if it had gone to Woodham's at Barry it would have surely been snapped up very quickly for preservation. *John Wiltshire*

THIS PAGE CENTRE The remains of rebuilt Bulleid pacific 'West Country' locomotives Nos 34032 *Camelford*, 34005 *Barnstaple*, 34009 *Lyme Regis* and 34026 *Yes Tor* were photographed on 18 November 1967 at Buttigieg's scrapyard in Newport Docks. The locomotives have been cut up by the scrapyard to carefully remove the copper fireboxes, which for large locomotives in 1967 could reach a scrap value of £1,300. They may however be in for a shock as Bulleid Pacifics were built during wartime austerity and they have welded steel fireboxes! *John Wiltshire*

THIS PAGE BOTTOM Original 'West Country' Pacifics Nos 34015 *Exmouth* and 34019 *Bideford* are seen at Cashmore's, Newport Docks, on 9 September 1967. No 34015 was withdrawn from Salisbury in April 1967, and No 34019 from Nine Elms in February of the same year. *John Wiltshire*

TOP The remains of BR Standard 2-6-2T 4MT tanks Nos 84006 and 84005 rest at Buttigieg's Newport yard on 20 August 1966. No 84006 was withdrawn from traffic in October 1965 and sent to the scrapyard from Leicester. No locomotives of this class were sent to Woodham's at Barry. *John Wiltshire*

ABOVE Fairburn '4MT' tank No 42247, GWR No 6856 *Stowe Grange* and BR Standard 2-10-0 '9F' No 92230 stand together at Cashmore's, Newport, on 9 April 1966. *John Wiltshire*

TOP Southern Railway 'S15' class No 30837 was withdrawn from traffic in September 1965 from Feltham and is seen here at Cashmore's scrapyard, Newport, on 20 August 1966. *John Wiltshire*

ABOVE SR 'Q1' class No 33020, diesel shunter No 15202, LMS 'Black Five' No 45418 and another 'Q1', No 33027, are seen at Cashmore's, Newport, on 20 August 1966. *John Wiltshire*

TOP LMS Fowler '3F' 0-6-0T No 47629 awaits its fate at Buttigieg's Newport yard on 3 February 1968. The locomotive was withdrawn from traffic in September 1967 at Westhouses near Mansfield. *John Wiltshire*

ABOVE LMS '8F' No 48255 and other locomotives stand in Buttigieg's yard on 9 July 1967. Note the rebuilt Bulleid Pacifics in the background; Nos 34005 *Barnstaple*, 34009 *Lyme Regis*, 34017 *Ilfracombe*, 34026 *Yes Tor* and 34032 *Camelford* were all present in the yard on that day. *John Wiltshire*

A long line-up of GWR locomotives just arrived at Cashmore's at Newport Docks for scrapping on 13 April 1962. The locomotives listed by John Wiltshire were Nos 5509, 5549, 7772, 5770, 8760, 9720 and 8451.
John Wiltshire

GWR pannier tank No 9642 is photographed at the R. S. Hayes scrapyard at Bridgend on 5 July 1968. This locomotive was not scrapped, but was purchased by the South Wales Pannier Group and moved to Maesteg Colliery, where it gave occasional brake van rides over NCB track in the early 1970s. The locomotive moved on to the now closed Swansea Vale Railway, then subsequently on to the Dean Forest Railway in 1998. Presently the locomotive is dismantled and under major overhaul for use on the Gloucestershire & Warwickshire Railway. *John Wiltshire*

Bulleid 'Pacific' No 34087 *145 Squadron* and BR Standard 5MT Nos 73118 and 73043 stand on the scrap line at Cashmore's, Newport Docks, in the late summer of 1968. No 73118 was cut up on 21 September 1968. *Peter Brabham collection*

51

4 | Woodham's scrapyard at Barry
The 1960s

The remarkable Woodham's scrapyard story at Barry Docks began at 5.20am on 25 March 1959 when four ex-GWR locomotives, Nos 5312, 5360, 5392 and 5397, were towed from Swindon Works to Barry Docks after being purchased from British Railways for scrap by Woodham Brothers.

Dai Woodham and his brother realised that the scrapping of steam locomotives by British Railways would not last for ever, so throughout the 1960s their company continued to purchase small batches of locomotives, which were then towed to Barry Docks by BR. These locomotives then gradually accumulated at various redundant sidings around the docks until the last batch of locomotives arrived in September 1968. In total, 297 steam locomotives arrived at Barry to be cut up for scrap by Woodham Brothers. Of these, six small steam locomotives also came by lorry from the War Department. Woodham Brothers also purchased four diesel locomotives, which also add interest to the story.

Woodham Brothers also cut up thousands of redundant British Railways coal trucks, wagons, oil tankers, diesel brake tenders and guards vans during the 1960s and 1970s. As a consequence the company only got around to cutting up 84 steam locomotives, leaving 213 as a reserve for when the wagon contracts dried up. The key factor in this remarkable story was the large number of available derelict railway sidings in the western part of Barry Docks on which to store the locomotives. Another factor was that Woodham Brothers was renting the sidings from Barry Docks, and was only being charged a peppercorn rent. If the company had paid a substantial rent for the sidings, it would not have made any economic sense to store the locomotives for three decades.

The accompanying graph shows that Woodham Brothers had bursts of activity in the 1959-65 period cutting up locomotives. The vast majority cut up were small ex-GWR tank locomotives, although they did cut up two large Bulleid 'Pacifics', Nos 34045 *Ottery St Mary* and 34094 *Mortehoe*, together with one BR 9F 2-10-0 freight locomotive, No 92232. Most of the metal from Woodham Brothers was sent to a steel works at Briton Ferry for recycling, although the wagon axles were sent to Europe to be extruded to make wire. The copper fireboxes, brass fittings and bronze bearings were separated out and sold at premium prices.

There were more than 100 locomotive scrapyards in the UK that scrapped thousands of steam locomotives throughout the 1960s. Many, such as Cashmore's in Newport, with restricted siding space, were cutting up locomotives within a week of their arrival. Only one scrapyard in the UK operated the practice of buying in a long-term reserve of locomotives and storing them to cover a lull in wagon contracts.

Initially in the early 1960s Woodham's scrapyard purchased former GWR locomotives that were being displaced from service by the introduction of diesel locomotives and diesel multiple units, the drop in coal traffic, and line closures in Wales and the West of England.

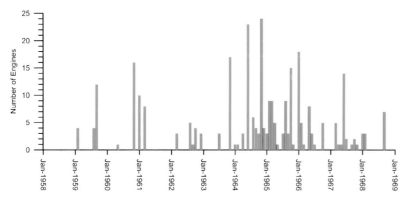

Locomotive arrivals for scrap at Barry Docks

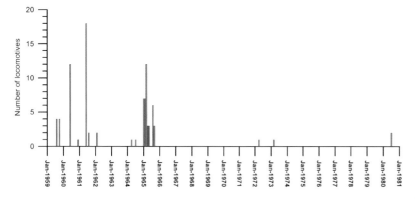

Steam locomotives cut up by Woodham Brothers

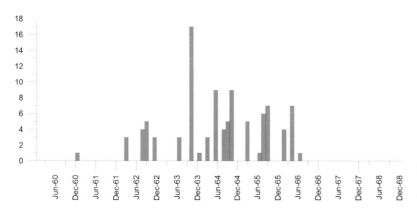

BR (GWR) preserved loco arrivals at Barry scrapyard

Until 1964 the withdrawn steam locomotives were stored on the old redundant coal sidings at the western end of Barry Docks, in areas known as the Main Yard and West Pond sites. By 1964 the Main Yard sidings were full and Woodham Brothers secured more space in the redundant high-level coal tip-sidings above the pump house, in an area that became known as the Top Yard. By the end of 1965 virtually all former GWR locomotives running on British Railways had been scrapped. However 1964-66 was the period of the sudden withdrawal of former Southern Railway locomotives. In particular, the closure of lines such as the Somerset & Dorset (1966) and the former London & South Western lines in the West Country such as those to Bude and Padstow (both 1966), together with electrification of the line to Bournemouth (1967), displaced more of the magnificent Bulleid 'Pacifics'. More than half of the 150 Bulleid 'Pacifics' were scrapped in South Wales, with 28 ending up at Woodham Brothers.

The last locomotives to arrive at Barry were a batch of seven in October 1968, comprising LMS Nos 48151 and 48305, BR Standard Nos 76077, 76079, 76084 and 92212, and the only LNER locomotive, No 61624. This former London & North Eastern locomotive came from Colwick, Nottinghamshire, where it had been used and abused working as a stationary boiler carriage heating unit.

The last bastion of steam in the UK was in the North West of England in the Liverpool to Carlisle district, and the final locomotive acquisitions by Woodham Brothers, between 1965 and 1968, comprised former LMS and British Standard locomotives from that area. The last regular steam-hauled main-line train on British Railways was on 11 August 1968, regular steam haulage ending with the famous 'Fifteen Guinea Special' from Liverpool to Carlisle and return. Of the four locomotives involved on that day, Nos 44781, 44871, 45110 and 70013, the two 'Black Fives' were purchased privately and No 70013 became part of the National Collection; only No 44871 was scrapped.

After 1968 the collection of more than 200 steam locomotives residing in Barry Docks was hard not to notice. The location of the southern end of the scrapyard sidings was adjacent to the main car park of the popular tourist resort of Barry Island and the lines of locos were also clearly visible from trains crossing the British Railways branch line. The popularity of Barry Island Butlins as a holiday destination in the late 1960s and 1970s meant that the lines of scrapped locomotives themselves became a major tourist attraction.

The start of the great locomotive preservation story began in September 1968, at the same time as the last batch of locos arrived. Woodham Brothers first received an enquiry to purchase ex-Southern No 31618. At that time the company was actually prohibited from reselling the intact locomotives in a clause of the contract it had signed with BR.

The 'Midland 4F Preservation Society' was a group of enthusiasts from the Lancashire area who in 1965 had tried to purchase an example of an ex-Midland 4F 0-6-0 locomotive direct from British Railways. They were quoted a purchase price of £2,000 by BR, with a seven-day deadline for a choice of two LMS examples still being used as shunters in Crewe Works. The high cost (the average UK

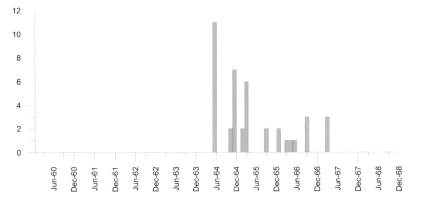

BR (Southern) preserved loco arrivals at Barry scrapyard

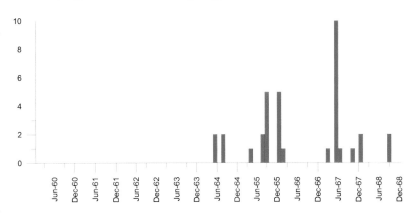

BR (LMS) preserved loco arrivals at Barry scrapyard

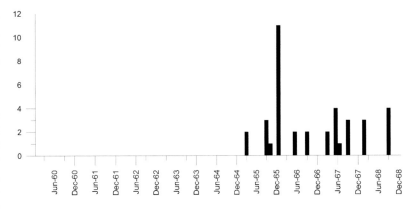

BR Standard preserved loco arrivals at Barry scrapyard

annual salary was around £1,300 in the late 1960s) and very short deadline were impossible to meet. Then the society found out that 4F No 43924 was still in existence at Woodham Brothers' scrapyard and, after an encouraging mechanical inspection at Barry, they tried to purchase the locomotive. However, because Woodhams had signed a contract with BR that locomotives it had purchased could not be resold unless cut up as scrap metal, it was not possible; eventually the contract had to be changed before any intact locos could be sold. The society had to approach Mr Cheetham, the BR scrap sales controller, for permission to purchase, and at first this was refused. After two years of negotiations with BR by the Association of Railway Preservation Societies (ARPS), the sale was finally agreed and LMS No 43924 was purchased for a scrap value of

Last BR shed allocations of surviving Woodham locomotives

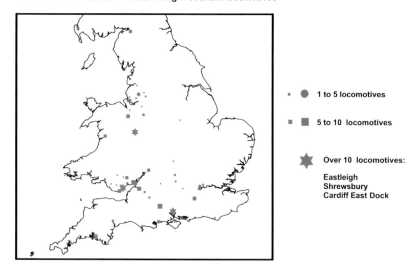

exception to this was LNER 'Pacific' No 4472 *Flying Scotsman*, which was purchased privately by Alan Pegler in 1962 and allowed to run charter trains over the BR network until 1968, when it went on a promotional tour of the USA.

After the success story of the preservation of the Talyllyn narrow-gauge line in Wales in the 1950s, the first standard-gauge preserved line in the UK was the Bluebell Railway in East Sussex in 1960. Gradually more preservation centres and steam depots developed throughout that decade, becoming home to a small number of steam locomotives either purchased direct from British Railways before the end of steam or smaller tank engines acquired from industries such as the National Coal Board. These centres, with their dates of opening, included:

Bluebell Railway	1960
South Devon Railway (Dart Valley Railway)	1965
Severn Valley Railway	1967
Great Western Society, Didcot Railway Centre	1967
Buckinghamshire Railway Centre, Quainton Road	1968
Birmingham Railway Museum, Tyseley	1968
Keighley & Worth Valley Railway	1968
Great Central Railway, Loughborough	1969
Steamtown Carnforth	1969
Kent & East Sussex Railway	1970

£2,500. In September 1968 it was towed by train from Barry at a cost of £500 to the Keighley & Worth Valley Railway.

This had now opened the door for many subsequent locomotive purchases. In January 1969 a second locomotive, former Southern Railway No 31618 left Barry for the Kent & East Sussex Railway. The third and last locomotive to leave in the 1960s was GWR 'Mogul' No 5322, to be restored by a branch of the Great Western Society at a site adjacent to the recently closed GWR Caerphilly Works.

Back in the late 1960s a problem with purchasing a main-line locomotive was the question of storage. Apart from a few locomotives in the National Collection such as *City of Truro*, which were occasionally brought out of the museum to run special trains in the 1960s, preserved steam locomotives were generally seen as polished static museum exhibits. The

The growth of these preservation centres and heritage railways in the late 1960s fuelled the appetite of many railway enthusiasts to purchase a locomotive from Woodham Brothers and restore it to working order. The great exodus of steam locomotives from Barry for preservation began in earnest in the 1970s, which is covered in the next section of this chapter.

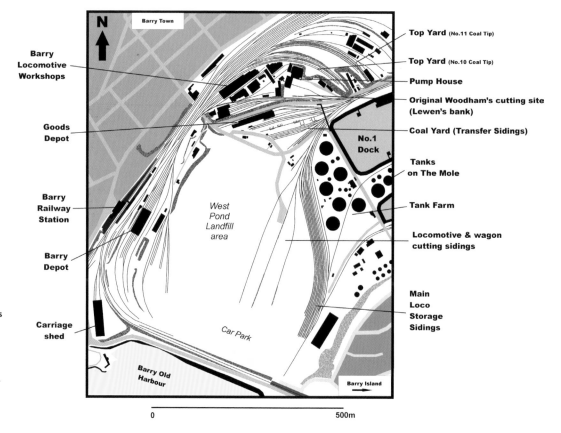

This site plan of the western part of Barry Docks highlights the areas of interest relating to the story of Woodham's scrapyard. The various locations of locomotives photographed over the 1959-90 period are outlined in red.

ABOVE **This enlargement of an aerial photograph of the infilled West Pond and locomotive works area of Barry Docks is dated 1966. The West Pond landfill is now complete and tracks are laid on top. The buildings of the Barry Railway works are still extant, as they were last used for wagon repair in 1965. The lines to the goods shed are also still in use. At this time locomotives were being accumulated in small batches and the Main Yard was becoming full. Locomotives were also being stored on the derelict sidings to the coal tips, which became known as the Top Yard. On the three cutting sidings on the West Pond site can be seen a line of War Department tank engines. The original Woodham's locomotive cutting site at Lewen's Bank, next to the pump house, had been abandoned and the tracks lifted by this time.** *Air Photo Unit, Welsh Assembly Government*

LEFT **Woodham Brothers' first scrapping site at Lewen's Bank beside the old Barry Railway Works is seen here in the early 1960s. In the far background a newly introduced DMU can be seen running over the island branch line.** *John Woodham collection*

The accompanying map illustrates the last recorded sheds to which the surviving locomotives from Woodham's scrapyard were last allocated. The main geographical areas from which the locos were obtained were:

- Former GWR and BR Standard locomotives from the local South Wales to Gloucester area
- Former GWR and BR Standard locomotives from Mid Wales (Shrewsbury-Machynlleth-Wrexham triangle)
- Former GWR and BR Standard locomotives from along the Severn Tunnel-London corridor
- Former Southern Railway locomotives displaced from the Bath-Southampton-Bournemouth area
- Former LMS and BR Standard locomotives from the North West (Liverpool) area

Apart from these general pockets of regional allocations, there were also other random locations such as various small sheds in the South West of England and South London sheds, together with the only ex-LNER locomotive, which was obtained from Colwick in the East Midlands.

The furthest depot to send locomotives to Barry scrapyard was Carlisle Kingmore, which provided five.

FACING PAGE TOP Hand-dismantling of a steam locomotive by the Woodham Brothers scrapping crew in the early 1960s. The white fluff on the ground is probably asbestos. *John Woodham collection*

FACING PAGE BOTTOM GWR 'Prairie' No 4164 was cut up by Woodham Brothers in December 1960. *John Woodham collection*

RIGHT GWR Churchward 2-6-0 No 5392 was the first locomotive to be cut up by Woodham Brothers at Barry Docks in February 1959. *John Woodham collection*

This fine line-up of GWR locomotives was recorded by the photographer as Nos 5552, 5557, 5794, 9468, 7722 and 5558 at Barry Docks on 25 February 1961. Sadly, all these locomotives were cut up by Woodham's for scrap in the autumn of 1965. *John Wiltshire*

GWR pannier tank No 9491 stands on the scrap line at Woodham Brothers, Barry, on 25 February 1961. This locomotive from Swansea was cut up in March 1965 together with 19 other members of the '94XX' class. *John Wiltshire*

TOP GWR pannier tank No 5422 resides on the scrap line at Woodham Brothers on 5 February 1961. This fine little GWR tank, last allocated to Oswestry, was cut up in February 1965. *John Wiltshire*

ABOVE This line-up of ex-War Department locomotives at the West Pond site on 14 September 1963 comprises Longmoor Military Railway (LMR) locomotives Nos 108, 178 and 203, together with three other WD locomotives, Nos 106, 119, 130, which all arrived in Barry in 1963 and were reported to have been scrapped on site by March 1965. *John Wiltshire*

ABOVE Ex-War Department No WD203 is captured en route to Barry scrapyard from Longmoor Camp, Hampshire, in July 1963. *John Wiltshire*

This War Department 0-6-0 saddle tank is seen at the West Pond site, Barry Docks, on 1 February 1964.
John Wiltshire

GWR 'Prairie' tanks Nos 5182 and 5547 at Barry Docks in 1964. No 5182 was cut up by Woodham Brothers in July 1964, No 5547 in March 1965. *Peter Brabham collection*

ABOVE GWR 'Prairie' tanks Nos 5521 and 4561, at Barry Docks in 1964, both showing damage to their front ends. Unlike the locomotives in the previous picture, by a throw of the dice both these locomotives survived the scrapyard to return to steam in 2006 and 1989 respectively. No 5521 would go on to pull the 'Orient Express'! *Peter Brabham collection*

LEFT LMS 'Jubilee' class 4-6-0 No 45699 *Galatea* is seen at Barry Docks on 7 June 1965, just after arriving at the scrapyard. During 15 years there the locomotive deteriorated into a total wreck, with a cut driving wheel and no tender. It was purchased in 1980 and disassembled for spare pa rts for sister locomotive *Leander*, based at that time on the Severn Valley Railway. In 1990, the component parts were purchased by the West Coast Railway Company, and miraculously *Galatea* will return again to main-line working order, possibly by 2013. *John Wiltshire*

Hawksworth 0-6-0 pannier tank No 9488 was built in 1952 by British Railways from a Great Western design. It worked in Bristol, Reading and various sheds in South Wales, and was withdrawn from Radyr shed in April 1965. It was then sold on to R. S. Tyley at Barry Docks, where it was used on track-lifting contracts until September 1965, in which month it was scrapped at Cadoxton. This photograph is undated, but must have been taken during the six months of its working period at Barry Docks. *Hedley Davies*

WOODHAM'S SCRAPYARD AT BARRY: THE 1960s

TOP Little did the father and son know, looking at GWR No 5972 *Olton Hall* and BR 'Merchant Navy' No 35029 *Ellerman Lines* at Barry Docks in 1966, that 45 years later *Olton Hall* would become one of the most famous steam engines in the world! *Ellerman Lines* met a strange fate, being cut in half as an educational exhibit at the National Railway Museum, York. *Rod McKay*

ABOVE Southern Railway 'Q' class No 30541 and 'West Country' No 34105 *Swanage* were photographed at Barry Docks on 7 June 1965. No 30541 was the only member of its class to survive into preservation, and is found today at the Bluebell Railway in East Sussex. *John Wiltshire*

ABOVE Rebuilt SR 'Merchant Navy' No 35005 *Canadian Pacific* is captured in the sunshine on beautiful Kodak slide film in late 1965 at Barry Docks, after withdrawal from Weymouth shed in September 1965. The last marks of hand-polishing are still visible on the paintwork, but the nameplate and coupling rods have been removed before being towed to Barry.
C. Aldred, Peter Brabham collection

LEFT SR 'West Country' class No 34039 *Boscastle* was withdrawn from Eastleigh in May 1965 and arrived in Barry in September. Here it is captured by the photographer soon after its arrival. *C. Aldred, Peter Brabham collection*

A line-up of locomotives withdrawn by British Railways in 1964, seen in the Top Yard sidings in 1965. In the foreground are two Maunsell 'U' class 2-6-0 locomotives Nos 31806 and 31618, and above them are LMS '8F' No 48431 and one of the two Fowler '7F' locomotives sent to the scrapyard from Bath.

C. Aldred, Peter Brabham collection

TOP Withdrawn steam locomotives gather in the Top Yard beside the Barry Railway workshops, in a slide dated 19 May 1964. The Fowler '7F' 2-8-0 in the background must have just arrived at Woodham Brothers' sidings. GWR 0-6-2T No 6622 (based at Merthyr shed) is seen working in the foreground; it would be cut up at Buttigieg's, Newport, in December 1964. *John Wiltshire*

ABOVE An unidentified GWR '56XX', withdrawn and stored beside Barry Railway workshops in 1966. *Peter Brabham collection*

LMS 'Jubilee' class No 45690 *Leander* is in the Top Yard at Barry on 25 May 1966. The locomotive had arrived in the yard in June 1964 and would leave in May 1972. *Peter Brabham collection*

A fine gathering of ex-GWR and ex-Southern locomotives in the Top Yard on 15 May 1966. Passing in the background is a 'merry-go-round' coal train for Aberthaw power station. *Peter Brabham collection*

An unidentified GWR '41XX' class 'Large Prairie' in the Top Yard, *circa* 1966. The BR lined livery is still visible. *Peter Brabham collection*

TOP GWR 'Large Prairie' No 4110, seen at Barry on 15 May 1966, had arrived eight months earlier from Severn Tunnel Junction shed. *Peter Brabham collection*

ABOVE BR Standard '9F' 2-10-0 No 92207 and 'West Country' No 34072 *257 Squadron* stand together at Barry Docks on 7 June 1965. No 92207 had arrived in the yard only three months earlier. *John Wiltshire*

ABOVE This line-up of newly arrived withdrawn locomotives from the Liverpool area, outside the goods shed at Barry Docks on 18 May 1967, includes Nos 47279, 46447, 42968 and 47298. *Les Ring*

RIGHT Newly arrived from Crewe, BR Standard No 78019 stands outside the goods shed on the same day. *Les Ring*

A line-up of newly arrived withdrawn locomotives outside the goods shed on 20 May 1967. The photographer noted the numbers as 47324, 42859, 92085, 75069, 47406, 47493, 78059, 78019 and 46512. *John Wiltshire*

RIGHT **Also on 18 May 1967, newly arrived from Crewe, BR Standard No 78059 stands at Barry Docks.** *Les Ring*

BELOW **Newly arrived single-chimney BR Standard 9F 2-10-0 No 92085 poses at Barry on 20 May 1967 after arriving from Birkenhead shed, only 10 years after it was built. Sadly, the locomotive was cut up in July 1980.** *Les Ring*

BELOW **Newly arrived from Eastleigh, Southampton, is BR Standard 4-6-0 No 75079, photographed on 25 May 1966.** *Peter Brabham collection*

ABOVE Unique BR Standard Pacific No 71000 *Duke of Gloucester* stands outside Barry Docks goods shed in December 1967. The locomotive was withdrawn in 1962 and put in store for preservation as part of the National Collection. It was subsequently decided that only its cylinders and valve gear were to be removed for technical display at the Science Museum, London. The rest of No 71000 was sold for scrap to Woodham Brothers, but it was actually delivered by mistake to Cashmore's yard in Newport. Luckily the mistake was spotted and 'the Duke' arrived at Barry in October 1967. *John Wiltshire*

RIGHT LMS 0-6-0 No 43294 at Barry Docks on 1 June 1968. This locomotive would be the first to leave Woodham's scrapyard for the Keighley & Worth Valley Railway, having spent the shortest time in the scrapyard of any locomotive, 2 years and 11 months. *John Wiltshire*

RIGHT Southern Railway 2-6-0 No 31618 at Barry Docks on 18 December 1968. This would be the second locomotive to leave the yard for preservation, in January 1969. *Les Ring*

BR Standard No 78018 stands in the Main Yard at Barry Docks on 17 September 1968. *Peter Brabham collection*

GWR 'Castle' No 5029 *Nunney Castle*, with a Hawksworth flat-sided tender, is seen in the Top Yard at Barry in 1968, having arrived in June 1964. *Chris Ravenscroft*

GWR 'Castle' No 7027 *Thornbury Castle* was also in the Top Yard, having also arrived in June 1964. *Colour-Rail*

Another June 1964 arrival was GWR 'Castle' No 5043 *Earl of Mount Edgcumbe*, seen in the Top Yard *circa* 1967. *Peter Brabham collection*

Southern Railway No 31806 at Top Yard, Barry Docks, *circa* 1967

Peter Brabham collection

Southern Railway 'West Country' No 34070 *Manston* in the Main Yard at Barry on 15 August 1966.

Peter Brabham collection

TOP This undated photograph of the Main Yard shows GWR 'Prairie' No 5539 and No 34028 *Eddystone*. No 5539 would spend 26 years in the scrapyard and is still unrestored today. *Hedley Davies*

ABOVE GWR 'Large Prairies' Nos 4160 and 4121 stand back to back with GWR 'Manor' class Nos 7821 *Ditcheat Manor* and 7827 *Lydham Manor* in the background in 1968. *Chris Ravenscroft*

LMS 'Crab' No 42859 and seven other locomotives are newly arrived at Barry Docks for scrap on 29 May 1967. It's every boy's dream to stand on the footplate! *John Wiltshire*

Diesel-electric No D8206 (later known as Class 15) stands in Barry Docks on 5 October 1969. It lasted only a few months in the yard, having been reported scrapped by 1970. Built by the Yorkshire Engine Co in 1958 and first allocated to Bow in East London, it had a very troublesome 800bhp Paxman engine and was sent for scrap from Stratford, London, in April 1969.
John Wiltshire

Virtually intact BR Standard '9F' locomotive No 92085 waits in Barry Main yard on an unknown date. Sadly, this fine heavy freight locomotive would last only until July 1980 before being cut up on site.
Peter Brabham collection

LMS No 53808 is seen in Barry Docks on 5 October 1969, having arrived from Bath in June 1964, two years before the closure of the Somerset & Dorset line from Bath to Bournemouth in March 1966, where it was a regular and well-photographed performer.
John Wiltshire

These virtually intact GWR pannier tanks are chalk-marked as Nos 4668 and 4612 in Barry Docks on an unknown date *circa* 1965. The number 4668 is probably wrong, as that locomotive was reported as being cut up in Bynea, Llanelli, in November 1965. GWR No 3738 is a likely candidate, as records show that it arrived in the yard with No 4612 in September 1965.
Peter Brabham collection

Intact GWR Collett 0-6-0 pannier tank No 9681 stands in the Main Yard on an unknown date. Built in 1949, it spent all its working life in the South Wales valleys, arriving at Barry scrapyard in 1965, reputedly under its own steam from Cardiff East Dock shed. It would leave Barry in 1975 for preservation by the Dean Forest Railway, returning to steam in 1984.
Peter Brabham collection

BR Standard Pacific No 71000 *Duke of Gloucester* has now moved to the Main Yard, and was photographed on an unknown date in the late 1960s.
Peter Brabham collection

Maunsell 'N' class 2-6-0 No 31874 was withdrawn from Exmouth shed in March 1964. This photograph was taken in the Top Yard in March 1968, and shows a still virtually intact engine; it had already been at Woodham's scrapyard for four years and the salty sea air was taking its toll on the paintwork. No 31874 would remain at Barry for another six years before being purchased for preservation on the Mid Hants Railway, where it took only three years to restore it again to working order.
Peter Brabham collection

A general view of more than 25 ex-GWR locomotives lined up in the Top Yard on 27 March 1969.
Peter Brabham collection

In this southerly view over the large number of locomotives lined up in the Main Yard on 29 March 1969, the black girder bridge of the Barry Island branch line is clearly visible in the background. *Peter Brabham collection*

By the end of the 1960s the Main Yard at Barry Docks was full of more than 200 withdrawn locomotives waiting to be cut up. This dramatic digitally restored 35mm slide image, taken on 20 March 1969 from the top of a locomotive cab looking north, shows the Main Yard sidings at full capacity. The overspill locomotives lined up in the Top Yard behind the pump house are also visible in the far distance. Of note are lines of locomotive tenders in the coal yard separated from their engines; these tenders were subsequently sold to a steelworks where their chassis were used as steel ingot carriers. This image clearly shows why Barry Docks became a magnet for railway preservationists over the next two decades. *Peter Brabham collection*

This was the view greeting holidaymakers and railway enthusiasts arriving at Barry Island station by DMU in the mid to late 1960s. Lines of more than 200 withdrawn locomotives are clearly visible from the railway embankment. The photo is undated, but was taken in the winter, as demonstrated by the ice and the lack of any cars and buses in the main island car park in the foreground. On the skyline the many blue cranes around Barry Docks are still in existence. The picture also shows how accessible the locomotives were to visiting enthusiasts and the general public. *Hedley Davies*

Woodham's scrapyard at Barry
The 1970s

The 1970s was the frenetic decade of locomotive preservation in the UK, with a large number of new heritage railway schemes being created all around the UK, and Barry scrapyard locomotives were in great demand to provide steam locomotives for them. In the early 1970s preservation societies could cherry-pick the most mechanically sound locomotives from Woodham Brothers' scrapyard for their restoration projects; some were virtually mechanically intact. The whole exercise was very costly, however; after purchasing the locomotive from Woodhams for £3000-£5000, a further £500 was required for transportation, then the funding of a major overhaul (£50,000 to £100,000) to return the locomotive to steam.

The accompanying graph shows a continual stream of locomotives leaving the yard throughout the 1970s. The burst of activity around 1973-74 relates to the introduction of VAT in the UK, which overnight added an extra 10% to locomotive purchase prices. Many deals were finalised just before the VAT introduction date, although the locos many not have actually left the scrapyard until many months later. Over the 1970s, with increasing scrap metal prices and tax, the cost of a Barry locomotive trebled. At its peak, Barry scrapyard contained more than 200 locomotives worth £1 million in scrap value alone. Locomotives were always sold by Woodham Brothers for scrap value, which was not easy to calculate, due to the concealed internal copper firebox and non-ferrous bearings and pipes.

Between 1968 and 1976 locomotives were often towed out of Barry by rail to sites with main-line access, such as the Severn Valley, Dart Valley and Tyseley. After 1976 all locomotives left the docks on the back of a heavy-haulage low-loader. Wynns of Newport and Mike Lawrence of Burnham in particular were well accustomed to delivering 80 tons of scrap metal to restoration sites all over the UK. Just getting out of Barry Docks on a heavy-haulage truck was quite a task as the main dock entrance was via a low tunnel. Locomotives had to make a circuit of the dock then pull up the steep hill onto the island before returning to

the mainland over the causeway road and the climb up out of Barry Town. This was all before the building of the M4 motorway west of Newport, so the abnormal load had then to negotiate its way through the Cardiff suburbs.

In the 1970s the scrapyard became a magnet for the artistic photographer. It was near compulsory to photograph the engines using grainy monochrome film, and shots of Barry scrapyard would regularly appear in art-house magazines. Thousands of railway enthusiasts visiting the scrapyard in the 1970s liked to take photographs and wander up and down the tight lines of locomotives making lists of the engines present. In October 1973 the Urie S15 Preservation Group published the first 'Barry List' pamphlet, the proceeds being ploughed back into their engine. This opened a debate as to exactly which engines were in the yard, as some were misidentified, which had already left for preservation, and the numbers of engines Woodham Brothers had actually scrapped. Through dialogue with other enthusiasts and the research of Roger Hardingham and the late Martin Beckett, the 'Barry List' developed and reached its 10th edition in 2010 (a decade after the last loco left Barry); it is considered as being the definitive list of engines that were present at Woodham Brothers. Most locomotives were easily identifiable by their painted numbers; however, the former GWR locomotives had been stripped of their brass cabside plates and smokebox numbers, so identification was made by the numbers stamped on the wheelsets. Even then there were later surprises; when dismantled for restoration, GWR No 4983 *Albert Hall* turned out to be No 4965 *Rood Ashton Hall*. This is not surprising, as many locomotives had interchanged frames, wheels and boilers at the end of steam, and convention dictates that the number of the locomotive frames defines the locomotive.

A remarkable number of standard gauge heritage railway line projects were started during the 1970s all over the UK:

Battlefield Line	1970
Dean Forest Railway	1971
Caerphilly Railway Society, Caerphilly Works	1971
Isle of Wight Railway	1971
East Somerset Railway, Cranmore	1972
Strathspey Steam Railway	1972
Cambrian Railway, Oswestry	1972
Dartmouth Steam Railway (Torbay Steam Railway)	1972
Tanfield Railway	1973
Mid Hants Railway	1973
North Norfolk Railway	1973
North Yorkshire Moors Railway	1973
Midland Railway Centre, Butterley	1973
Steamport, Southport	1973
Lakeside & Haverthwaite Railway	1973

Locomotive departures from Woodham's Barry for preservation 1970s

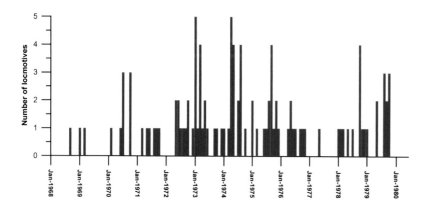

Nene Valley Railway	1974
Colne Valley Railway	1974
Gwili Railway	1975
Llangollen Railway	1975
Swanage Railway	1975
Peak Railway	1975
West Somerset Railway	1976
Telford Steam Railway	1976
Southall Railway Centre	1976
Avon Valley Railway	1977
Swindon & Cricklade Railway	1978
Embsay & Bolton Abbey Railway	1979

Throughout the early 1970s advertisements would appear in railway magazines inviting people to form a new society to preserve a particular Barry locomotive. In May 1973 the Secretary of new 71000 (Duke of Gloucester) Preservation Society attended the AGM of the Association of Railway Preservation Societies to seek membership, but the proposal was laughed out of the room as nobody believed it could possibly be serious! After six months of money-raising the society only had £124 in the bank. However, it invited £100 shares in a restoration company and within three month had raised the full £4,950 asking price.

Many of these new heritage railway lines developed rapidly and have now become major tourist attractions in the UK, bringing millions of pounds into the local economy. Only a very small number failed to flourish, mainly because their sites were redeveloped.

Throughout the 1970s many hundreds of people all over the UK spent their unpaid spare time restoring Barry scrapyard locomotives and returning them back to working order. In those pioneering days, conditions were often primitive and there are many examples of major express locomotives being restored outdoors inside plastic tents.

Gradually infrastructure projects improved conditions on the heritage lines, providing restoration sheds with heavy lifting and much improved repair facilities.

The 1970s saw four locomotives cut up at Barry: two diesel locomotives in 1970 (blue-liveried diesel-hydraulic 'Warship' No D600 and diesel-electric No D8206) and two steam locomotives (BR Standard No 76080 in 1972 and GWR No 3817 in 1973).

Notable locomotives that left the yard for preservation during that decade to service the new heritage lines included:

- GWR No 4983 *Albert Hall*, the first GWR 'Hall' class to leave, in 1970
- GWR No 5051 *Earl Bathurst*, the first 'Castle' class loco to leave, also in 1970; all five of the GWR 'Castles' left the yard during the decade
- GWR No 7827 *Lydham Manor*, the first 'Manor' class loco to leave, in 1970
- S&DJR 7F No 53808, which left in 1970; classmate No 53809 left in 1975
- SR No 34092 *City of Wells*, the first 'West Country' locomotive to leave, in 1971
- LMS 'Jubilee' No 45690 *Leander*, which left in 1972
- GWR No 6024 *King Edward I*, leaving in 1973
- SR No 35005 *Canadian Pacific*, the first 'Merchant Navy' loco to leave, in 1973
- BR No 71000 *Duke of Gloucester*, in 1974
- BR 9F No 92240, the first 2-10-0 to leave Barry, in 1978

In total, 105 steam locomotives left Barry scrapyard for preservation during the 1970s, and throughout the decade many of them were returned to working order. By 1979 half of the locomotives had left Barry for preservation centres around the UK.

A close-up from an aerial photograph of the Top Yard in July 1971 shows 33 steam locomotives in three lines on the old curved tracks that once led to the now derelict dock coal tips. The buildings of the Barry Railway works have been demolished, but the chimney of the pump house survives to this day. The original Lewen's Bank cutting area of Woodham's scrapyard is now abandoned.
Cardiff University, Earth Sciences photo archive

This is the Main Yard and West Pond site, also in July 1971. The cutting up of wagons and brake vans is in full swing while long lines of steam locomotives and trucks await their turn in the Main Yard. GWR 'Prairie' No 5572 can be seen alone in the coal yard waiting to be moved off to Didcot. No 34016 *Bodmin* has also been pulled out of the Main Yard to stand alone in a siding.
Cardiff University, Earth Sciences photo archive

ABOVE This general view of Woodham's Main Yard in Barry Docks in June 1970 can be matched up with the previous aerial photograph. The locomotive in the left foreground is GWR No 7802 *Bradley Manor*, and in the centre is LMS '4F' No 44123. The latter left Barry in 1981 for the Avon Valley Railway at Bitton, Bristol, where it is undergoing a long-term restoration. *Rod McKay*

LEFT This photograph was taken by the 11-year-old author on his Kodak Instamatic in 1972. It was pure magic to be able to wander around the yard with your father and brother climbing over the locomotives, although the cramped photographic conditions of the Main Yard at this time are obvious.
Peter Brabham

This image was taken in the early 1970s for NatWest bank publicity purposes and features Dai Woodham (on the right) showing his bank manager, Cyril Jones, around Woodham's Main Yard. Ivatt tank No 41313, built in 1952, is a rather interesting Barry engine, in that it was purchased by the Ivatt Locomotive Trust and moved to Quainton Road, Buckinghamshire, in 1975. However, it was stored in a shed at the museum site virtually untouched for more than 30 years because it was essentially just a source of spares for the Trust's other engine, No 41298, purchased direct from BR in 1967. In 2006, both locomotives were taken via the ferry to the Isle of Wight Railway for restoration and future use on the island's heritage railway. *John Woodham collection*

Southern Railway 'West Country' No 34016 *Bodmin*, seen on 5 September 1970, has been pulled out of the Main Yard for preservation. However, it will not leave until July 1972 for Quainton Road, Buckinghamshire. It was then moved on in 1976 to the then fledgling Mid Hants Railway where it was restored to working order under a plastic tent in 1979. *Les Ring*

TOP BR Standard '5MT' No 73156 in the Main Yard in June 1970. The locomotive left Barry in 1986 and is now in the later stages of a long restoration at the Great Central Railway, Loughborough. *Rod McKay*

ABOVE BR Standard '2MT' No 78019 is also seen in the Main Yard in June 1970. The locomotive left in March 1973 for the Severn Valley Railway, but returned to steam on the Great Central Railway in 2004. *Rod McKay*

North British 'Warship' No D600 *Active* wears BR blue livery with a full yellow front. The locomotive was introduced in 1958 and spent most of its working life between Plymouth and Exeter. In 1967, all the class moved to Swansea Landore for freight work. The locomotive was withdrawn from Plymouth Laira in December 1967, towed to Barry with classmate No D601, and cut up in 1970. *Class 20 Society*

BELOW 'Warship' No D601 *Ark Royal* is still in BR green livery at Barry scrapyard in June 1970; it was cut up in June 1980. *Rod McKay*

BELOW BR Standard '4MT' No 80079 is seen in June 1970; it would leave in 1971 for the Severn Valley Railway. *Rod McKay*

LMS (Midland Railway) '4F' No 44123 in the Main Yard in June 1970. *Rod McKay*

BELOW This line-up of Bulleid Pacifics in 1971 includes 'West Country' No 34010 *Sidmouth* and 'Merchant Navy' No 35010 *Blue Star*. *Peter Brabham collection*

FACING PAGE TOP A hard to identify GWR 'Hall', most likely No 5952 *Cogan Hall* stands in the Main Yard in 1973. *Peter Brabham*

FACING PAGE BOTTOM A view of locomotives in the Top Yard in the early 1970s. Urie 4-6-0 'S15' No 30506 is subject to a restoration appeal by Roger Hardingham, as can be seen by the notice tied on its smokebox. Roger raised funds for restoring this locomotive by publishing editions of the definitive 'Barry List'. *Peter Brabham collection*

A GWR 'Castle' in the depths of the Main Yard in June 1970. The white smokebox brackets suggest that it is No 7027 *Thornbury Castle*. *Rod McKay*

Another view of the collection of locomotives arranged on the curved redundant Top Yard lines in the early 1970s. *Peter Brabham collection*

FACING PAGE TOP GWR 'Small Prairie' No 4566 is seen on 25 July 1970, just prior to leaving for the Severn Valley Railway. *John Wiltshire*

FACING PAGE BOTTOM GWR 'Small Prairie' No 5541 was photographed on the same day; it would leave in 1972 for the Dean Forest Railway. *John Wiltshire*

Two GWR 'Castle' class locomotives, Nos 5029 *Nunney Castle* and 5080 *Defiant*, are seen on 25 June 1974. By that time both had been ransacked by treasure hunters and metal thieves. Despite its condition, No 5080 would be towed out of Barry by diesel locomotive in tandem with GWR Nos 4160 and 5367 in August 1974 bound for Birmingham Railway Museum, Tyseley, at a maximum speed of 15mph. *Nunney Castle* would leave in 1976 for the Great Western Society at Didcot. *Peter Brabham collection*

A side view of No 5080 *Defiant*, taken on the same day. *Peter Brabham collection*

ABOVE GWR 'Small Prairie' No 5521 in 1973. *John Wiltshire*

Seen on 7 September 1971, GWR 0-6-2T No 5643 will soon be leaving the yard, initially for Cwmbran, Monmouthshire; it was subsequently restored in the Lake District. *John Wiltshire*

ABOVE On 5 September 1970, cosmetic preservation of GWR 'Small Prairie' No 5572 by the Great Western Society has begun. *John Wiltshire*

The cosmetically restored No 5572, photographed on 10 January 1971, would leave that October for the Great Western Society Taunton Branch, later moving to Didcot. *John Wiltshire*

A general view of the overcrowded Main Yard taken from the cab of pannier tank No 9466 on 26 April 1972. *Peter Brabham collection*

GWR 2-8-0 No 2885, minus a tender, stands in the Main Yard in the early 1970s. The engine left in 1981, purchased by the Great Western Preservation Group at Southall depot in west London. It was subsequently cosmetically restored at Tyseley Museum and stands on display at Birmingham Moor Street station. In 2012 it was put up for sale by the group and purchased by a consortium with the intention of returning it to steam at Tyseley. *Peter Brabham collection*

GWR 2-8-0 heavy freight locomotive No 2857, built to haul heavy goods trains across the GWR network, undergoes cosmetic preservation in 1972. Sixteen of this type of locomotive were sent to Barry scrapyard, and No 2857 was the first of them to be purchased for preservation. It was bought for use on the Severn Valley Railway, and left Barry in August 1975.
Peter Brabham collection

GWR 2-8-0 No 3862 in 1972; the heavy freight locomotive would languish in the scrapyard until 1989. *Peter Brabham collection*

GWR Nos 6023 *King Edward II* and 6024 *King Edward I* are seen in 1974. The story of how two GWR 'King' locomotives ended up in Barry scrapyard is the stuff of legend. The story is that *King Edward I* and *King Edward II* were withdrawn at Swindon Works and placed on the scrap line. Dead weights were required for bridge testing in South Wales and these two locomotives were chosen. After the bridge testing was finished they were to be scrapped at Briton Ferry, Neath, until it was realised that 'King' class locomotives were not allowed west of Cardiff, so they were re-routed to Woodham's at Barry and given dispensation to travel down the Barry branch line to arrive at the docks in December 1962.

Both Peter Brabham collection

Hagley Hall is being cosmetically and mechanically prepared for removal from the scrapyard in January 1973, still with a broken handrail, and the photographer's children being used as a scale. No 4930 has the later flat-sided Hawksworth tender. The locomotive left Barry Docks in tandem with GWR locomotives Nos 4141, 4930 and 7819, towed by a diesel bound for Kidderminster on the Severn Valley Railway. *Hagley Hall* returned to steam in 1979. *Hedley Davies*

GWR 4-6-0 No 6024 *King Edward I* is being prepared for removal from Woodham Brothers' yard with some cosmetic paintwork now applied. The locomotive was purchased for £4,000 by the 6024 King Preservation Society and taken out of the yard in March 1973 to the Buckinghamshire Railway Centre at Quainton Road. The restoration took 16 years, culminating in a return to steam on 2 February 1989. *King Edward I* returned to main-line steam action on 15 April 1990 and has been a regular main-line performer ever since. By comparison, on the right is diminutive LMS 0-6-0 'Jinty' tank No 47298, which left Barry in July 1974 for Southport; it underwent a relatively rapid return to steam by 1979 and also participated at the Rainhill 150 celebrations in 1980. In more recent years No 47298 has appeared in disguise as 'Thomas the Tank Engine'. *Hedley Davies*

Bulleid 'Merchant Navy' class locomotive No 35018 *British India Line* stands in the cramped Main Yard sidings in the early 1970s. The locomotive left the scrapyard in 1980 for the Mid Hants Railway; it subsequently moved on to a workshop site in Portland. In June 2012 *British India Line* was purchased by West Coast Rail Co, and moved to their Carnforth base with the aim of long term restoration to mainline standard to add to their pool of charter locomotives.
Peter Brabham collection

TOP **Somerset & Dorset/LMS Fowler '7F' No 53809 in the Top Yard on 4 March 1973.** *Peter Brabham collection*

ABOVE **A 1972 portrait of LMS 'Jubilee' class No 45690** *Leander,* **just prior to its purchase and removal to Derby Works for rapid professional overhaul and return to steam by August 1973.** *Peter Brabham collection*

ABOVE Southern Railway Maunsell 'S15' No 30847 and Urie 'S15' No 30499, photographed on 26 May 1973. *Peter Brabham collection*

GWR No 7812 *Erlestoke Manor* is seen in 1974, just prior to removal to the Severn Valley Railway. *Peter Brabham collection*

LMS 'Black Five' No 45379, seen here on 26 May 1973, would leave in 1974 for Bristol. *Peter Brabham collection*

TOP 'Black Five' No 45491 and 'West Country' No 34070 *Manston* stand in the line of locomotives in the Main Yard in the early 1970s. After private purchase, No 45491 left Barry in 1981 and restoration began at the Midland Railway Centre at Butterley; it is now in its final stages at the Great Central Railway at Loughborough. The locomotive is planned to return to steam by 2013/14. *Peter Brabham collection*

ABOVE GWR No 5952 *Cogan Hall* in the Main Yard sidings *circa* June 1973. The locomotive was originally purchased with the aim of restoration on the Gloucestershire Warwickshire Railway. However, it was subsequently acquired as a source of GWR parts for the *Betton Grange* new-build project on the Llangollen Railway. *Peter Brabham collection*

TOP GWR 4-6-0 No 7828 *Odney Manor* in the Main Yard sidings *circa* 1973. Seven 'Manor' locomotives arrived at Woodham Brothers in the summer of 1966, having worked trains in Mid Wales and along the Cambrian coast until withdrawal. All seven have been returned to steam, as they are an ideal size and weight for most heritage lines. *Odney Manor* was the last example of the class to leave Barry scrapyard, in June 1981. *Peter Brabham collection*

ABOVE No 6990 *Witherslack Hall* shows signs of loving care and attention by the Witherslack Hall Locomotive Society in the Main Yard *circa* 1973. The locomotive left the yard in November 1975 for a successful restoration at the Great Central Railway, Loughborough, in 1986. *Peter Brabham collection*

Southern Railway No 34058
Sir Frederick Pile on 26 May 1973.
The rebuilt Bulleid 'Battle of Britain'
'Pacific' arrived at Barry in April
1965 after withdrawal from Eastleigh
Works in September 1964. Attached
to No 34058 is GWR No 7821
Ditcheat Manor. *Peter Brabham collection*

BR Standard '4MT' No 76079, also
photographed on 26 May 1973; the
locomotive would leave in 1974 for
Southport. *Peter Brabham collection*

Six months after this picture was
taken on 5 September 1970, LMS
No 46521 left for the Severn Valley
Railway. *Les Ring*

ABOVE LMS No 48518 is seen in the Main Yard on 26 May 1973. Although apparently quite intact, the locomotive would deteriorate and remain in the scrapyard until 1988. Its ultimate fate was dismantling to provide parts for other locomotive restoration projects. *Peter Brabham collection*

LMS Stanier Mogul No 42968, seen on 29 March 1973, would leave that December for the Severn Valley Railway. *John Wiltshire*

GWR pannier tank No 9466, photographed in June 1975, is undergoing cosmetic restoration by Dennis Howells. It would leave three months later for Quainton Road, Buckinghamshire. No 9466 is the only '94XX' class locomotive of the 20 that came to the Barry scrapyard that was not cut up. *Peter Brabham collection*

TOP Southern Railway 'Battle of Britain' class No 34081 *92 Squadron*, June 1975.
Peter Brabham collection

ABOVE By 20 May 1973, the 71000 Duke of Gloucester Preservation Society had started cosmetic restoration of BR Standard Pacific No 71000 *Duke of Gloucester*, adding a new set of smoke deflectors courtesy of one of the yard's '9F' locomotives. By this time the locomotive had unfortunately lost its tender, as it had been sold to a steelworks for use as an ingot carrier. *Peter Brabham collection*

ABOVE Rather battered-looking GWR Mogul No 9303, seen on 23 March 1975, left in September for the Severn Valley Railway. To the rear, in grey primer, is GWR pannier tank No 9644, and behind is green 'Warship' No D601 *Ark Royal*. *John Wiltshire*

TOP The sole former LNER locomotive at Barry scrapyard, LNER Thompson 'B1' class 4-6-0 No 61264 is seen in 1975, before leaving for preservation at the Great Central Railway in 1976. Although externally the locomotive looks mechanically sound, due to the abuse it took in the last few years of its life working as a stationary boiler, internally the boiler was in a very poor condition, requiring more than a quarter of a million pounds of firebox and boiler repairs to return it to steam. *Andrew Wiltshire*

TOP Southern Railway Maunsell 'S15' class No 30847 in the Main Yard in the mid-1970s. *Peter Brabham collection*

ABOVE Southern Railway Maunsell 'U' class No 31638 stands in the Main Yard, also some time in the mid-1970s. *Peter Brabham collection*

Seen on 26 May 1973, GWR 2-8-0T No 5239 has moved up to Barry depot and is just about to leave for restoration at the Dart Valley Railway. *Peter Brabham collection*

LEFT GWR 0-6-2T No 5619 is loaded onto a Wrekin Roadways low-loader in Barry scrapyard in May 1973 for its journey to Telford, Shropshire. It was purchased by Telford Development Corporation for the Telford Horsehay Steam Trust, and was restored to working order by 1981 with a ten-year boiler certification. It then remained dormant from 1991 until a second major overhaul was completed by the Flour Mill in 2008, and it can now be seen out on hire to many heritage lines. *Hedley Davies*

FACING PAGE TOP LMS 'Crab' class No 42859, also photographed on 26 May 1973. Two of the 245 'Crabs' built by the London Midland & Scottish Railway and introduced in 1926 made it to Woodham Brothers. *Peter Brabham collection*

FACING PAGE BOTTOM 'Crab' No 42765 left Barry in 1978; here the locomotive is waiting in the coal yard, and behind is LMS '8F' No 48151, which today is a main-line certified engine based at Carnforth. *Andrew Wiltshire*

FACING PAGE TOP The preservation society paid £4,950 for the unique No 71000 *Duke of Gloucester* with a '9F' tender. Here 'the Duke' leaves Barry Dock on 24 April 1974 for Loughborough after 6½ years in the scrapyard. *John Wynn collection*

FACING PAGE BOTTOM 'The Duke' was hauled to Loughborough on the back of a heavy haulage trailer owned by the Newport firm of Wynns. Due to two low railway bridges at both the dock town entrances, locomotives leaving Barry Dock had to take a circuitous route up onto the island, including a very steep 1 in 7 climb up Dock Road. *John Wynn collection*

RIGHT No 71000 only just made it under the railway bridge on the outskirts of Cardiff on its long trip to Loughborough. *John Wynn collection*

BELOW GWR No 7822 *Foxcote Manor* leaves Barry Island for Oswestry on a Wynns heavy haulage wagon in January 1975. *John Wynn collection*

Southern Railway 'West Country' class No 34092 *City of Wells* left the scrapyard in October 1971 for the Keighley & Worth Valley Railway.
Peter Brabham collection

Southern Railway 'West Country' class No 34105 *Swanage* in June 1975. The locomotive left the scrapyard in March 1978 for the Mid Hants Railway.
Peter Brabham collection

In this view of the Main Yard at Barry Docks in the summer of 1978, GWR pannier tank No 4612 is in the foreground and Bulleid Pacific No 34072 coupled behind.
Peter Brabham

TOP A general view of Main Yard, also in the summer of 1978, with BR No 73096 on the left. By 1978, approaching 50% of the Barry locomotives had left the yard for preservation. *Peter Brabham*

ABOVE A view of the Main Yard on 10 June 1978, showing BR Standard 4MT 2-6-0 No 76077 and 'Merchant Navy' class No 35011 *General Steam Navigation*. No 76077 did not leave Barry until 1987 and is undergoing long-term restoration at the Gloucestershire Warwickshire Railway. No 35011 remains unrestored, having donated one of its driving axles to the restoration of No 34046 *Braunton* on the West Somerset Railway. *Peter Brabham collection*

TOP Southern Railway 'Merchant Navy' class No 35027 *Port Line*, summer 1978.
Peter Brabham

ABOVE Southern Railway 'Merchant Navy' class No 35022 *Holland America Line*, also seen during the summer of 1978. Presently the unrestored locomotive is in store at Southall. *Peter Brabham*

GWR 2-8-0 No 2807, summer 1978. Despite its rather basic condition here, it is now a regular service engine on the Gloucestershire Warwickshire Railway. *Peter Brabham*

GWR No 7802 *Bradley Manor*, summer 1978. *Peter Brabham*

Also photographed in the summer of 1978, GWR pannier tank No 3612 left in December for the Severn Valley Railway, where it was dismantled to supply spare parts for pannier engines on the SVR and Llangollen Railways. *Peter Brabham*

TOP BR Standard No 75079, summer 1978. *Peter Brabham*

ABOVE BR diesels Nos D6122 and D601 in the yard, summer 1978. D6122 was a diesel-electric locomotive (later Class 21) built by North British in 1959, and had a troublesome working life in Scotland. In 1967 it was moved to Hither Green, London, to be used as a dead weight to practise re-railing exercises, before being sold for scrap to Woodham's, arriving in June 1968. It was scrapped in 1980. *Peter Brabham*

BR Standard '9F' No 92207 and GWR
No 7903 *Foremarke Hall*, summer
1978. *Peter Brabham*

BR Standard 9F No 92134 and
No 7802 *Bradley Manor* stand among
the plethora of scrap metal at the
West Pond site in summer 1978.
Peter Brabham

BR Standard No 80098, summer 1978.
Peter Brabham

THIS PAGE TOP LMS Ivatt '2MT' 2-6-0 No 46428 at the end of the line at Main Yard in the winter of 1978. The locomotive would leave Barry in 1979 originally for the Strathspey Railway in Scotland. Re-sold in 1987, the unrestored locomotive is now in store on the East Lancashire Railway. *Peter Brabham*

THIS PAGE CENTRE Ivatt 2-6-2T No 41312 is captured on 25 June 1974. The locomotive was initially purchased by the Caerphilly Railway Society in 1974, but was sold on in the 1990s and is now based at the Mid Hants Railway, having returned to steam in 2000. *Peter Brabham collection*

THIS PAGE BOTTOM GWR 'Large Prairie' No 5193 is isolated at the northern end of the Main Yard on 8 August 1977. The 'Prairie' tank left Barry in 1979 for Southport, but was later purchased by the West Somerset Railway for conversion into a hybrid GWR 2-6-0 tender locomotive and given a brand new GWR number, 9351. *Peter Brabham collection*

FACING PAGE TOP GWR 2-8-2T No 7200 was photographed on 2 September 1978. Although the locomotive has been pulled out of the Main Yard for transportation, it will not leave for Buckinghamshire until 1981. *Albyn Austin*

FACING PAGE BOTTOM BR Standard '9F' No 92214, No 7927 *Willington Hall* and 4979 *Wootton Hall* at the Coal Yard on 2 September 1978. *Albyn Austin*

FACING PAGE TOP The deteriorating condition of GWR No 6023 *King Edward II* is obvious on 2 September 1978. Note the graffiti on the locomotive, giving up hope of ever restoring this once magnificent locomotive. *Albyn Austin*

FACING PAGE BOTTOM Southern Railway No 34073 *249 Squadron*, also photographed on 2 September 1978. *Albyn Austin*

THIS PAGE TOP GWR 'Large Prairie' tank No 5193 features in this general view of the West Pond site at Barry Docks on 2 September 1978. *Albyn Austin*

THIS PAGE CENTRE Southern Railway Nos 34046 *Braunton* and 34070 *Manston* on 2 September 1978; both locomotives are now restored to pristine working order on the West Somerset Railway and Swanage Railway respectively. *Albyn Austin*

THIS PAGE BOTTOM A general view of the West Pond site in 1977 with diesel No D6122 at the head of the line. *Peter Brabham collection*

ABOVE Standing back to back amongst the West Pond site debris in 1977 are BR Standard '9F' No 92219 and Southern Railway 'West Country' No 34101 *Hartland*. *Peter Brabham collection*

RIGHT The sad remains of LMS No 45699 *Galatea* in 1977; the torched driving wheel was thought at the time to stop it ever being preserved. By this time *Galatea* had lost its tender, purchased by the group preserving LMS No 45491. *Peter Brabham collection*

BR Standard '5MT' No 73082 *Camelot*, seen here in the late 1970s, left the yard for the Bluebell Railway in October 1979. *Peter Brabham collection*

ABOVE A southerly panoramic view taken from Barry Town looking over the West Pond area *circa* 1977, with Barry Island fairground and promenade in the background. Many locomotives are now occupying the West Pond sidings, standing among the debris of wagon-cutting. The Butlins camp and its cable-car system are clearly visible on the left skyline.
Hedley Davies

RIGHT In the 1970s, many of the locomotives deteriorated badly, exposing the asbestos boiler cladding. GWR 2-8-0 No 3802 is in a terrible condition on 8 August 1977, but despite this it left the yard in 1984 for preservation, initially at Bodmin but subsequently completed at the Llangollen Railway. *Peter Brabham collection*

RIGHT No 3802's sister engine, No 3855, is seen on 25 June 1974. The locomotive was purchased in 1987 for the Blaenavon Railway, but remained unrestored in the outdoor yard there for more than a decade.
Peter Brabham collection

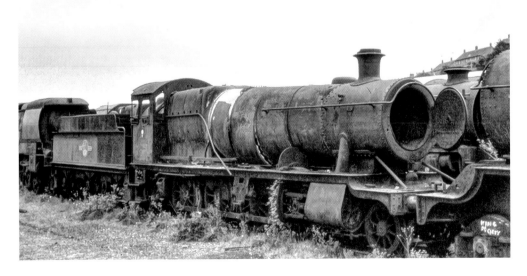

Woodham's scrapyard at Barry
The 1980s

At the start of the 1980s there were around 100 steam locomotives still present at Woodham's scrapyard at Barry Docks. The Top Yard had been abandoned by this time and all remaining locomotives had been consolidated down at the Main Yard and West Pond sites. The scrapyard was now entering the last part of the cycle. The accompanying graph shows the number of locomotives present in Woodham Brothers' scrapyard over the complete 1958-1990 period of its existence in Barry Docks.

In July 1980 Woodham Brothers rocked the railway preservation world by scrapping two steam locomotives, GWR 'Prairie' No 4156 and BR Standard 9F No 92085. Two diesel locomotives, Nos D601 and D6122, were also cut up in 1980, but these went comparatively unnoticed, although there is much interest today in preserving the diesel pioneers. Woodham Brothers' explanation for resuming cutting was that they had a lull in wagon-cutting contracts, so to keep their employees busy they just cut up the first two locomotives in the scrap line that had not been reserved for purchase. This focussed the attention of preservationists on the fate of the remaining Barry locomotives. Those left in the yard were duplicates of locomotive classes already preserved, so their preservation was really a matter of their suitability for use on developing heritage lines, not their historical uniqueness. There were at this time mixed feelings about restoring the remaining Barry locomotives; some felt it would distract money and effort from ongoing restoration projects.

Until 1980, for every loco that Woodham's sold to a preservation society 50% of the profit between the re-sale price and the original purchase price from British Railways was returned to BR. Woodham's was also paying the docks board £1.32 per loco per week, which worked out at around £6,000 per year for all the locos.

By the 1980s the state of the steam locomotives left in the yard was generally poor, as those in the best mechanical condition had left in the 1970s. Many parts of the remaining locos had also been purchased (or stolen) to support many locos already preserved. The engines were constantly deteriorating; the longest resident in the yard, GWR No 5553, would stand in the salty sea air for 28 years. However, in the early 1980s there was a state of anarchy in the scrapyard, and many parts were being removed by professional thieves, as copper, gun-metal, white-metal and brass were very valuable. Twenty-three people were prosecuted for metal theft from the yard. On one occasion, Dai's son John found human fingers in the axle box of a wagon that had been illegally jacked up, but the jack had obviously slipped just as the thief was pulling out the bearings. Many loco parts had also been illegally removed by weekend 'work parties' preserving other locos in the yard, so a ban on work parties was enforced. The cab of BR Standard tank No 80072 disappeared overnight. Much of this theft and damage would be catastrophic to the future restoration potential of many locomotives. Dai Woodham was getting thousands of requests by letter and telephone for official yard visits. Different preservation societies were bickering over particular locomotives, which by the late 1980s could approach £10,000 in scrap value. One potential millionaire buyer landed in the yard by helicopter to view prospective locomotives.

Another problem was that the asbestos lagging was becoming exposed on many locomotives. In the summer of 1980 the Environmental Health Department issued a statement that no locomotive could leave the yard without either having its blue asbestos lagging professionally removed or being totally sealed in a plastic bubble while in transit. For many locomotives still in the yard that had already been purchased, this suddenly added an extra £1,000 for professional contractors to carry out the stripping task and disposal. Woodham Brothers also had to pay for asbestos removal for many of the unpurchased locos left in the yard, which becomes obvious in many late-1980s photographs that show locos with exposed boilers.

A further factor was that there were locomotives left in the scrapyard that had in the past become derailed while being shunted around because their wheel bearings had been removed. The quick solution carried out by Woodham's was to torch the driving wheels affected. Therefore any restoration of these locomotives would involve having to re-cast new driving wheels, which at that time was a daunting and expensive task. Two significant locomotives with severed driving wheels were GWR No 6024 King Edward II and LMS 'Jubilee' No 45699 Galatea, which had not been subject to preservation appeals.

Some locomotives were deemed to be too large and too heavy for use on heritage lines. Only two out of the ten former Southern Railway 'Merchant Navy' class locomotives

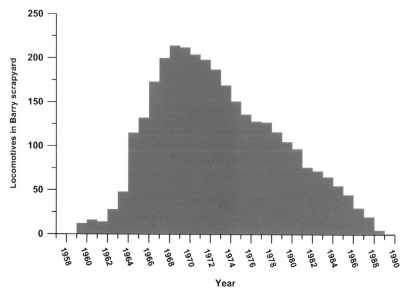

Number of locos present in Barry scrapyard by year

had been purchased in the 1970s, and the rest were proving unpopular as potential restoration projects.

A final problem was that the tenders of some locomotives were sold off to Briton Ferry steelworks to be cut down for use as ingot carriers. There were suddenly far more locomotives left in the yard than available tenders. Some old tenders were still in existence on the BR network in use as water tanks, and a few locomotive preservation groups secured suitable tenders by purchasing them direct from BR. Other preservation groups have had to construct brand new tenders from scratch, utilising various second-hand wheelsets.

The Barry Steam Locomotive Action Group (BSLAG) was formed with the aim of acting as a coordinating body between Woodham Brothers and all the various preservation societies and private individuals hoping to preserve a locomotive. Francis Blake played a big part in the story, acting as an intermediary between Dai Woodham and the many societies and individuals wishing to acquire a Barry locomotive. The aim of BSLAG was to preserve all the locomotives and not see any more cut up, which it did by lobbying Parliament and Government agencies. BSLAG was also supported by the Association of Railway Preservation Societies (ARPS) to raise the profile of Barry locomotives. All those left in the scrapyard were professionally assessed and all found to be potentially salvageable, given available funding. A definitive record of remaining locos and their various interested parties was compiled. The late railway enthusiast Robert Adley MP made speeches in Parliament about the long-term fate of the Barry locomotives. As a result of BSLAG raising the profile of the remaining locomotives and the possibility of them being cut up, many new potential locomotive owners and preservation groups were found. A detailed account of this period and the personalities involved is given in the 1987 book *The Barry Locomotive Phenomenon* by Francis Blake and Peter Nicholson.

By the mid-1980s the continued existence of the scrapyard was also in doubt as Dai Woodham was past retirement age and the redundant western part of Barry Docks was becoming a focus of potential redevelopment and regeneration. The derelict land, which had been near worthless for more than 20 years, could now be potentially sold off by Associated British Ports for supermarket and luxury housing developments.

Throughout the 1980s gradually more locomotives were purchased, and one by one they were moved to various sites around the UK. By the spring of 1987 the redevelopment plans for Barry Docks were progressing and Woodham Brothers would have to vacate the West Pond site and the remaining locomotives moved or scrapped by mid-1988. By the late 1980s the scrap-metal cost of a Barry locomotive was between £6,000 for a small tank engine and £9,500 for one of the remaining large tank or tender engines. However, this initial purchase price would, from experience, turn out to be actually only between 5% and 10% of the total cost of returning these now rusting hulks to steam.

From the 1980s to the present day new heritage railway projects have been developed around the UK, still creating

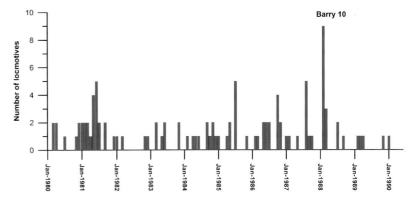

Locomotive departures from Woodham's Barry for preservation 1980s

a demand and providing restoration bases for unrestored Barry locomotives:

Plym Valley Railway	1980
Bo'ness & Kinneil Railway	1981
Gloucestershire Warwickshire Railway	1981
Pontypool & Blaenavon Railway	1983
East Anglian Railway Museum	1983
Northampton & Lamport Railway	1984
Swansea Valley Railway	1985
Bodmin & Wenford Railway	1987
Crewe Heritage Centre	1987
East Lancashire Railway	1987
Barrow Hill Railway Centre	1991
Weardale Railway	1993
Chinnor & Princes Risborough Railway	1994
Churnet Valley Railway	1996
Mid Norfolk Railway	1997
Vale of Glamorgan Railway	1997
STEAM, Swindon	2000
Ribble Steam Railway	2001
North Dorset Railway Trust, Shillingstone	2002
Garw Valley Railway	2006

In February 1988 South Glamorgan Council purchased ten locomotives that represented those with South Wales links. The 'Barry 10' locomotives were transported the 8 miles to the old headquarters of the Taff Vale Railway in Cardiff Bay, and there were ambitious plans to develop a Welsh National Railway Museum. Six unrestored Barry locomotives ended up at Blaenavon in another ambitious plan to develop a significant heritage railway in South Wales. Another major project at that time was a planned railway museum and restoration centre at Preston Park, Brighton. Southern 'Pacifics' Nos 34073 and 35009 and LMS 'Black Five' No 45293 were purchased and destined for this project, which sadly was never developed. One locomotive, GWR 'Prairie' No 5538, was donated by Dai Woodham for permanent display on the seafront at Barry as a tribute to the role Barry and Woodham Brothers had played in heritage preservation.

The 213th and last locomotive, GWR 'Small Prairie' No 5553, was privately purchased and moved off the Barry Docks site to Birmingham on 31 January 1990. This was effectively the end of the 31-year story of Woodham's scrapyard at Barry Docks. However, all over the UK locomotives were being restored and

North

In the early 1980s the yard was thinning out, allowing for more photographic opportunities. However, the locomotives were deteriorating badly due to the salty sea air, vandalism by souvenir hunters, and preservationists taking parts for other locomotives that had been rescued. Some of the casings were also becoming damaged, exposing the asbestos boiler and cylinder insulation. *Peter Brabham*

FACING PAGE TOP This enlargement of a 1979 aerial photograph of Barry Docks shows the West Pond site and the west end of No 1 Dock. By this period the Top Yard had been abandoned and the tracks lifted. The lines to the goods depot had also been lifted. The Main Yard is thinning out, and locomotives waiting to leave are lined up in the coal yard. The roofs of the two remaining diesel locomotives are clearly visible. Lines of wagons can be seen on the three cutting lines in the reclaimed West Pond landfill site. *Reproduced by permission of Ordnance Survey on behalf of HMSO © Crown Copyright 2011. All rights reserved. Ordnance Survey licence No 100020212*

FACING PAGE BOTTOM The 1980s began with the shock news that Woodham Brothers had scrapped two steam locomotives because the company had run out of wagons to keep its employees busy. The two locomotives were British Railways Standard '9F' No 92085 and GWR 'Large Prairie' No 4156, seen here partly dismantled in July 1980. This event sent shock waves through the preservation movement, focusing attention on rescuing the remaining locomotives. The driving wheels of No 4156 were purchased by the Severn Valley Railway and are in use today on another locomotive. *Peter Brabham*

LEFT Although Woodham's yard was a wonderful place for the railway enthusiast to wander around for hours, this image clearly shows the limited photographic opportunities within the lines. As can be seen, the path between the lines in the Main Yard is well worn by thousands of visitors. The southern end of the Main Yard was adjacent to the tourist car park for Barry Island and, with a constantly damaged fence, the temptation was just too great to go for a look around the steam engines. On more than one occasion Woodham employees had to rescue young lads who had got themselves stuck in the chimney of a steam engine! In the late 1970s Woodham's yard became one of Wales's top tourist attractions. John Woodham joked in conversation that they had missed a financial opportunity at that time to put up a steel fence around the yard and charge people for guided tours around the locomotives! *Peter Brabham*

The scrapyard closed in 1990 and later that decade the site was skimmed of surface contaminants, many emanating from the various hydrocarbon chemical tanks located around the docks, as well as asbestos from the cutting yards. Gradually the scrapyard site has actively undergone redevelopment, with the old Top Yard embankments and locomotive works sites being razed for industrial buildings, housing and a hotel. It was only in 2012 that the Main Yard and West Pond sites were being redeveloped, mainly due to the high costs of stabilising what is essentially industrial landfill on top of soft clays, dating back to its pre-industrial time as the Cadoxton River estuary.

continually returned to steam. In 2012, more than two decades later, many locomotive restoration projects are still coming to fruition. Numerous unrestored Barry locomotives are still scattered all over the UK at various preservation centres for long-term restoration, for use as spares for other working locomotives, or for ambitious plans to recreate long-lost steam engine classes.

Dai Woodham died at his home from lung cancer on 12 September 1994, aged 75. He had been awarded an MBE in 1987 for his services to the local community, setting up small business units in the docks. He left behind three sons and three daughters. Before his death he auctioned off nearly all of his railway artefacts, including his remaining locomotive nameplates.

Through Dai Woodham's sons, Woodham Brothers still has a presence at Barry Docks, managing business units for small companies. It would be nice to think that when the docks site is totally redeveloped, some tribute will be made to the company's huge legacy to the UK's industrial heritage preservation – street names such as King Edward I Avenue, Defiant Road, Duke of Gloucester Way, Leander Drive or Hartland View spring to mind. One unrestorable Barry locomotive could be placed on a plinth in tribute to the site's historical significance.

GWR 2-8-0 No 2874 left the yard in 1987, only to spend a further 22 years in the open at Blaenavon. The locomotive has now been sold to the West Somerset Railway as a long-term restoration project. It is seen here in January 1985, having been stripped of its asbestos lagging. *Andrew Wiltshire*

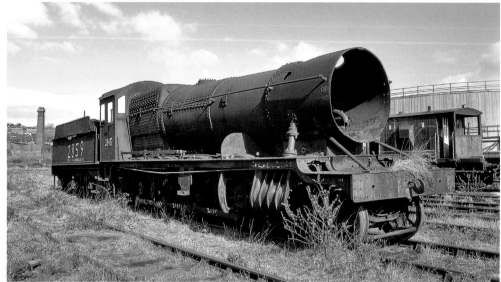

GWR 2-8-0 No 3845 was the penultimate locomotive to leave the yard, on 9 November 1989, with great ceremony. However, the locomotive's fate has not been secure, moving from Brighton to Swindon and finally to the Gloucestershire Warwickshire Railway, where its long-term restoration prospects are more promising. *Peter Brabham*

GWR 2-8-0 No 3850 left the yard in 1984 for the West Somerset Railway. Despite its poor condition, the locomotive was restored to steam in 2005 and became a regular on the heritage line. *Peter Brabham*

TOP GWR 2-8-0 No 3862 is seen in March 1985. The locomotive was the 211th to leave Barry, being moved in 1989 to the Northampton & Lamport Railway. Note the pile of BR station trolleys on the left. *Andrew Wiltshire*

ABOVE GWR 2-6-2T No 4115 left Barry in 1988 as one of the 'Barry 10' for the ill-fated Wales Railway Centre in Cardiff Bay. After being evicted from Cardiff Bay, the locomotives were put in store in a warehouse back in Barry and finally returned to Barry depot. The locomotive's long-term was to be broken up for doner parts in the summer of 2012. *Peter Brabham*

TOP GWR 2-8-0T No 4248 left the yard in 1986, originally for restoration in Essex. It was then moved to Swindon's STEAM museum, stripped down to its boiler and used in a diorama of locomotive overhauls carried out by women employed at the works during the Second World War. *Peter Brabham*

ABOVE GWR 2-8-0T No 4253 left the yard in 1987 with prospects of being restored in Wale s at Blaenavon. However, in 2011 the virtually untouched locomotive moved to the Kent & East Sussex Railway, to a group keen to **restore it.** *Peter Brabham*

GWR 2-8-0T No 5227 departed with great fanfare in 1988 as one of the 'Barry 10', to start a Wales Railway Centre in Cardiff Bay. The locomotive was broken up in the summer of 2012 to release donor parts for other GWR locomotive projects. *Peter Brabham*

GWR 2-6-2T No 5526 left the scrapyard in 1985, first for Gloucestershire, then Swindon, and finally the South Devon Railway. In 2008, the locomotive returned to steam on the heritage line in unlined BR black livery. *Peter Brabham*

GWR 4-6-0 No 4979 *Wootton Hall* left Barry for the North West of England in October 1986 after private purchase. Here it is seen in the scrapyard in January of that year. Today the unrestored remains of No 4979 can be seen by travellers on the Settle & Carlisle line as they pass through Appleby station. *Peter Brabham*

In 1987, GWR 2-6-2T No 5538 was given by Dai Woodham to the local council, which wanted to put a locomotive on display on Barry seafront. After a swapping of parts with sister locomotive No 5532, the cosmetically restored 'Prairie' was put on display from 1992 to 1997. It then moved to the Vale of Glamorgan Railway, but is now at the Dean Forest Railway. *Peter Brabham*

GWR 0-6-2T No 6686 left Barry in 1986 to become one of the ill-fated 'Barry 10'. *David Brabham*

GWR 2-6-2T 'Small Prairie' No 5553 was the 213th and last locomotive to leave Barry scrapyard on 31 January 1990, heading for Birmingham. As can be seen, the locomotive appeared to be in a very poor mechanical state, but thanks to Pete Waterman and the restoration expertise of Tyseley Railway Museum it was completely restored to steam and is now normally resident on the West Somerset Railway. *Peter Brabham*

TOP GWR No 6023 *King Edward II* in the yard in 1983. By this time the fate of the locomotive was looking more promising, despite its cut driving wheels. It would leave Barry in 1984 for Bristol Temple Meads station, sponsored by Harvey's of Bristol, and eventual restoration to steam in 2011 was achieved at the Great Western Society, Didcot. *Peter Brabham*

ABOVE After private purchase, GWR No 6984 *Owsden Hall* left Barry in 1986 for Oxfordshire. The locomotive is now under active restoration on the Gloucestershire Warwickshire Railway. *Peter Brabham*

TOP GWR 2-8-2T No 7200 left Barry in 1981 for the Buckinghamshire Railway Museum at Quainton Road, where the big GWR tank is under active but long-term restoration. *Peter Brabham*

ABOVE GWR 2-8-2T No 7229 departed from the scrapyard in 1984 for Plymouth, but later moved on to the East Lancashire Railway, where it was dismantled into parts. *Peter Brabham*

This 1981 view shows GWR pannier tank No 9629, 'Small Prairie' No 5553, and a line of other locomotives. After 20 years in the scrapyard, the sea air has worn away all paintwork to reveal the bare metal. No 9629 left Barry in 1981, the 100th departure. it was cosmetically restored at Steamtown, Carnforth, for display outside a Cardiff hotel. It is now under restoration on the Pontypool & Blaenarvon Railway. *Peter Brabham*

Southern Railway Urie 'S15' class No 30499 left Barry in November 1983 for the Mid Hants Railway, and is seen here in May 1985. Its boiler was removed and used to return sister engine No 30506 to steam.
Andrew Wiltshire

In 1987 Southern Railway 'S15' class No 30830 went from Barry to the Bluebell Railway. No 30830 was later re-sold to the North Yorkshire Moors Railway as a source of spares for two other locomotives of the same class, Nos 30825 and 30841. Having three ex-Barry locomotives of the same class on the same line means that it is much easier to maintain one of them in steam. *Peter Brabham*

ABOVE Southern Railway 'West Country' No 34007 *Wadebridge* left Barry in 1981 for Plymouth, subsequently moving to the Bodmin & Wenford Railway, where it was returned to steam in 2005. It is now resident on the Mid Hants Railway. *Peter Brabham*

RIGHT A close-up of Southern Railway 'Merchant Navy' No 35009 *Shaw Savill* in the early 1980s. The locomotive would rot away in the scrapyard for 25 years until what was left of it was removed in 1989. Its fate since has been insecure, moving from Brighton to Swindon Shopping Centre, and the remains are now in store at Ian Riley's workshop in Bury. *Peter Brabham*

Southern Railway No 34028 *Eddystone* left Barry in 1986 for a private site in Kent, where restoration commenced. *Eddystone* was then moved to Swanage, where it returned to steam in 2004. *Peter Brabham*

Rebuilt Southern Railway 'West Country' No 34046 *Braunton* left Barry in 1988 for the ill-fated Brighton Works project. It was then privately purchased and by 2008 had been restored to steam on the West Somerset Railway. *Peter Brabham*

Seen here in January 1986, Southern Railway No 34058 *Sir Frederick Pile* moved from Barry that July to the Avon Valley Railway at Bitton, Bristol. In July 2011 the locomotive was moved to the Mid Hants Railway to continue its restoration. *Andrew Wiltshire*

ABOVE The stencilling on No 34073 *249 Squadron* states that it was removed from Barry scrapyard on St David's Day (1 March) in 1984. However, the locomotive did not finally leave Barry until February 1988. The locomotive remains were originally destined for Brighton, but it ended up for many years in store on the Mid-Hants Railway. In 2006 it was moved to Ian Riley's Sworkshop at Bury, Lancashire, where it supplied donor parts for No 34072 following damage to its running gear. *Andrew Wiltshire*

LEFT Unrebuilt Southern Railway 'West Country' locomotives Nos 34073 *249 Squadron* and 34072 *257 Squadron* left the yard in 1988 and 1984 respectively. The latter was restored to steam at Swindon and ran on the Swanage Railway until its boiler certification expired. *249 Squadron* first moved to Brighton Works, but is now in store on the East Lancashire Railway. *Peter Brabham*

ABOVE Southern Railway 'Merchant Navy' No 35006 *Peninsular and Oriental S. N. Co.* left Barry in 1983 for the Gloucestershire Warwickshire Railway. This long-term restoration project is now reaching its final stages and the 'Merchant Navy' should be working again on the G/WR in the near future. This will be the third former Barry 'Merchant Navy' locomotive to return to steam of the ten that were in the scrapyard. *Peter Brabham*

RIGHT The remains of Southern Railway 'Merchant Navy' No 35009 *Shaw Savill*, seen here in May 1982, are presently in store in Bury. *Peter Brabham*

Southern Railway 'Merchant Navy' No 35025 *Brocklebank Line* left Barry in 1986 for the Great Central Railway, but the unrestored remains are now in store. *Peter Brabham*

ABOVE No 35011 *General Steam Navigation* is paired with a Great Western tender in full sunshine in 1988. The locomotive would become the last Bulleid Pacific left at Barry right up until March 1989, when it was moved to the ultimately unsuccessful Brighton Locomotive Works project. The locomotive has since moved to a site in Lincolnshire. *Peter Brabham*

RIGHT Rebuilt Bulleid 'Battle of Britain' No 34053 *Sir Keith Park*, seen here in 1983, was purchased privately and left Barry in 1984 for Hull. It subsequently became one of the pool of Bulleid Pacifics under restoration by Southern Locomotives Ltd, based at Swanage. The locomotive returned to steam in the summer of 2012 and was hired out on loan to the Severn Valley Railway. *Peter Brabham*

LMS 'Black Five' No 44901 left Barry in 1988 as one of the 'Barry 10', but in 2012 it is the subject of a restoration appeal and bound for the Gloucestershire Warwickshire Railway. *Peter Brabham*

TOP BR LMS 'Crab' 42859 in March 1985. The locomotive left Barry in 1986 and is now in a dismantled state at RAF Binbrook in Lincolnshire. It has been reported that the boiler of this locomotive is in a poor condition and would require a very expensive restoration back to steam. At the time of final preparation of this book the locomotive's future looks bleak, as the dismantled remains are under threat of being sold for scrap. Andrew Wiltshire

ABOVE LMS 'Black Five' No 45163 is caught in the setting winter sun in December 1983. The locomotive left Barry in 1987 and is now under restoration at the Colne Valley Railway. Andrew Wiltshire

TOP LMS 'Black Five' No 45337 left Barry in 1984 and, despite its terrible condition in this photograph, was restored to steam on the East Lancashire Railway. It has also worked on the North Yorkshire Moors and West Somerset Railways. *Peter Brabham*

ABOVE 'Black Five' No 45293 left Barry in 1986 and is currently under restoration on the Colne Valley Railway. *Peter Brabham*

TOP **Two 'Black Fives', Nos 44901 and 45337.** *Peter Brabham*

ABOVE **LMS Fowler '3F' 0-6-0T 'Jinty' No 47406 left Barry in 1983 and was returned to steam on the Great Central Railway in 2009.** *Peter Brabham*

ABOVE LMS '8F' No 48173 left Barry in 1988, initially for the Avon Valley Railway, but is now on the Churnet Valley Railway where it is in storage for future restoration. *Peter Brabham*

BELOW Having left Barry in 1985, LMS '8F' 2-8-0 No 48305 was restored to steam on the Great Central Railway at Loughborough. This locomotive was always a favourite for photography in the scrapyard, with the crying face drawn on its smokebox. *Peter Brabham*

BR Standard 4MT No 76084 has a very interesting restoration story. Painted in a bright red oxide, it was purchased from Woodham Brothers in 1983 for £7,500 by the late Phil Rollin, who had it delivered to the driveway of his house in Nottinghamshire. Mr Rollin carried out cosmetic restoration, but after he passed away his daughter sold the 59-ton locomotive to a restoration consortium and it was moved to Morpeth, Northumberland. Mechanical restoration started in the open air, but progressed more easily after a purpose-built shed was erected. At a cost of £350,000 the locomotive restoration is now in its final stages. The final push to completion is being helped financially by the North Norfolk Railway, where it will find a working home in 2013. *Peter Brabham*

TOP LMS '8F' No 48518 left Barry in 1988 as one of the 'Barry 10'. The locomotive is seen here in the yard in January 1986. After 20 years in store in South Wales, it was stripped and its component parts will now be used for both the Llangollen LMS 'Patriot' and the GWS Didcot 'County' new-build projects. *Andrew Wiltshire*

ABOVE BR Standard '5MT' No 73096 left Barry in 1985 for the Mid Hants Railway. The locomotive had been restored to steam by 1993 and has seen service on a number of heritage lines, and some main-line work, but is based on the Mid Hants Railway. *Peter Brabham*

TOP BR Standard 4MT No 76077 left Barry in 1987 for the Gloucestershire Warwickshire Railway, where it is stored in the long-term restoration queue. *Peter Brabham*

ABOVE BR Standard 4MT tank No 80072 is seen here in terrible condition, being overtaken by vegetation at Barry in 1986. In 1988, the locomotive left Barry for Swindon, then later went to the Llangollen Railway. It had been restored by the Standard Four Project by 2009 and is presently working at Llangollen, as well as often out on loan to many other UK heritage lines. *Peter Brabham*

TOP BR Standard '4MT' tank No 80104 left Barry in 1984 and can now be seen working on the Swanage Railway. *Peter Brabham*

ABOVE BR Standard '4MT' tank No 80150 left Barry in 1988 as one of the 'Barry 10'. After 22 years in store in South Wales, its remains have been moved to the Mid Hants Railway, being swapped for a turntable to be installed at Barry depot, where it will be used in the future to turn main-line steam locomotives. *Andrew Wiltshire*

TOP BR Standard '9F' 2-10-0 No 92219 was the youngest steam locomotive in Barry scrapyard, having been built in January 1960, the penultimate steam locomotive built by British Railways. After only five years in BR service around South Wales and Bristol, it was sent to Barry for scrap. Having spent another 20 years in the scrapyard, it left in 1985 for Peak Rail. The locomotive is now unrestored at the Midland Railway Centre, Butterley. *Peter Brabham*

ABOVE BR 2-10-0 No 92245 was the last of the seven '9F' locomotives in Barry scrapyard in 1988, and became part of the 'Barry 10'. It is seen here in the late 1980s going back to nature on the West Pond site. *Peter Brabham*

ABOVE This photograph was taken in 1988 when there were only a few locomotives left in the scrapyard, in stark contrast to shots from the 1960s. Here is GWR 2-8-0 5227 again, awaiting its move to the Wales Railway Centre in Cardiff Bay. Unfortunately this project never developed and more than two decades later the locomotive was back in Barry depot, still rusting away, until broken up for doner parts in the summer of 2012. *Peter Brabham*

LEFT Another final scrapyard image taken in 1988 outside the pump house. The locomotive on the left is 'Merchant Navy' No 35009 *Shaw Savill*, and the other is 'Battle of Britain' No 34073 *249 Squadron*, stripped of its casing. The locomotives left the scrapyard in 1988/89 and are both still unrestored. This location is now the site of Barry's new Premier Inn Hotel, and the pump house underwent structural restoration in 2012, hopefully ensuring its long-term future. *Peter Brabham*

5 Great Western Railway steam locomotives purchased from Barry scrapyard

In total, 98 former Great Western Railway locomotives were purchased from Barry scrapyard, and the types and numbers are listed below. Those locomotive numbers in **bold** have been returned to steam, but may currently be in store out of boiler certification or under overhaul.

0-6-0 pannier tank locomotives
3612 **3738 4612 9466** 9629 **9681 9682**

0-6-2 tank locomotives
5619 5637 5643 5668 **6619** 6634 6686 **6695**

2-6-2 'Small Prairie' tank locomotives
4561 4566 4588 5521 5526 5532 5538 5539 **5541 5542 5552 5553 5572**

2-6-2 'Large Prairie' tank locomotives
4110 4115 4121 **4141 4144** 4150 **4160 5164 5193 5199**

2-8-0 tank locomotives
4247 4248 4253 4270 **4277 5224** 5227 **5239**

2-8-2 tank locomotives
7200 7202 7229

2-6-0 tender locomotives
5322 7235

2-8-0 tender locomotives
2807 2857 2859 2861 2873 2874 **2885 3802 3803** 3814 **3822** 3845 **3850** 3855 3862

4-6-0 'Manor' class
7802 7812 7819 7820 7821 7822 7827 7828

4-6-0 'Hall' class
4920 4930 4936 4942 **4953** 4979 **4983 5900** 5952 5967 **5972 6960** 6984 6989 **6990 7903** 7927

4-6-0 'Castle' class
5029 5043 5051 5080 7027

4-6-0 'King' class
6023 6024

Without the invaluable contribution of the ex-Barry scrapyard locomotives to the heritage railway pool, we would have very few examples of standard gauge GWR locomotive classes preserved. Ignoring small shunting tank engines, the preserved GWR locomotives that largely were purchased direct from BR are:

TVR original locomotives	2	TVR No 28 (National Collection)/TVR No 85 (K&WVR) via the NCB
0-4-2 tanks	4	four of the diminutive '14XX' class
0-6-0 Pannier tanks	17	most were preserved via the NCB and six via London Transport
0-6-2 tank	1	No 6697 purchased for the Great Western Society (GWS), Didcot
Small 2-6-2 Prairie tank	1	No 4555 purchased privately
Large 2-6-2 Prairie tank	1	No 6106 preserved for the GWS, Didcot
0-6-0 tender locomotives	2	Nos 2516 'Deans Goods' (National Collection)/3205 'Collett Goods'
2-8-0 tender locomotive	1	No 2818 (National Collection)
4-4-0 tender locomotives	2	No 3440 City of Truro (National Collection)/'Dukedog' No 9017 (Bluebell)
4-6-0 'Star' class	1	No 4003 Lode Star (National Collection)
4-6-0 'Manor' class	1	No 7808 Cookham Manor preserved by GWS, Didcot
4-6-0 'Hall' class	1	No 6998 Burton Agnes Hall preserved by the GWS, Didcot
4-6-0 'Castle' class	3	No 4073 Caerphilly Castle (National Collection), No 4079 Pendennis Castle (GWS, Didcot) and No 7029 Clun Castle (Birmingham Railway Museum)
4-6-0 'King' class	1	No 6000 King George V (National Collection)

RIGHT **Great Western pannier tank No 9682 was one of the last of these ubiquitous GWR-designed locomotives to be built at Swindon Works in 1949, after nationalisation. The locomotive left Barry in November 1982 for the GWR preservation centre at Southall depot, and returned to steam in 2000. It was a regular performer on the Chinnor & Princes Risborough line, where it is seen on 22 June 2009. Its boiler certification expired at the end of that year and it is expected to return to steam again in 2011 after another major overhaul.** *Peter Brabham*

BELOW **Great Western pannier tank No 9861 was built in 1949 at Swindon Works and spent all its working life in the South Wales valleys. In August 1965 it steamed into Barry Docks under its own power and stayed there rusting until October 1975, when it was purchased and moved to the Dean Forest Railway. It returned to steam in 1984 and has seen regular use on the line for 25 years. In April 2011 it heads deep through the forest towards Parkend.** *Peter Brabham*

GWR No 9466 was one of 15 Hawksworth '94XX' class pannier tanks sent to Barry scrapyard in the early 1960s. Fourteen were cut up, but fortunately the sole survivor was purchased by Dennis Howells in 1975. It had a working life of only 12 years on British Railways, but since its restoration at the Buckinghamshire Railway Centre it has been seen all over the UK. It has been present at five of the eight London Transport 'Steam on the Met' events, and is seen here at Neasden depot in 1995 being prepared for a day's work on London Underground's Metropolitan Line. *David Brabham*

The Great Western '56XX' class 0-6-2 tanks were the final design of many types of 0-6-2Ts built to haul coal trains from pits in the South Wales valleys to the ports and steelworks. No 5619 was purchased from Barry in May 1973 by Telford Development Corporation as a heritage project in the Midlands town. It initially returned to steam in 1981, but spent a considerable period out of boiler certification in the 1990s. The locomotive has now again returned to steam and it usually seen out on hire to heritage railways. Here it is pictured at a Gloucestershire Warwickshire gala event pulling an exhibition freight train in May 2008. *Peter Brabham*

GWR No 5643 was built in 1925 and, after a life working in the South Wales valleys, was withdrawn to Barry in 1963. It was the 16th locomotive to be purchased from there, in 1971. It was initially intended for a new preservation centre based at Cwmbran near Newport, but after the failure of this project it was moved to the Lake District, first to Steamtown at Carnforth, then to the Lakeside & Haverthwaite Railway. Its slow restoration in the station car park could be viewed by passing tourists each summer. No 5643 finally returned to steam in 2005, and the magnificent results are seen here at Bewdley at a Severn Valley Railway autumn gala event in 2009. In 2012 No 5643 is undergoing a 10-year overhaul at the Ribble Steam Railway. *Peter Brabham*

GWR No 5637 spent 39 years working the South Wales valleys until withdrawal to Barry in 1964. A decade later it was purchased and moved to Tyseley Museum, Birmingham. It was then purchased by Thamesdown Council, Swindon, as a heritage project for the town, and moved to the Swindon & Cricklade Railway for restoration. The council then sold it on to the 5637 Preservation Group, which returned the locomotive to steam. On 4 July 2010, No 5637 is seen working on the East Somerset Railway. *Peter Brabham*

ABOVE GWR No 6619 is another '56XX' class locomotive that spent all its working life of 35 years in South Wales, spending a great deal of its time actually based at Barry depot. It was used to shunt locomotives around Barry Docks until its own withdrawal in 1963. Purchased privately in 1974, it moved to the North Yorkshire Moors Railway. In October 1984 it returned to steam and has been a regular service locomotive on the very popular heritage line ever since; here it is seen in 1984 approaching Goathland station. No 6619 has also appeared on loan to various preservation lines. In 2011 it was put up for sale by its owners. In 2012 the locomotive was purchased by a group of Kent & East Sussex Railway members for use on the heritage line. *Peter Brabham*

RIGHT GWR No 6695 is another '56XX' class 0-6-2T locomotive, withdrawn to Barry in 1964. It was built by Armstrong Whitworth in Newcastle under contract to the GWR. Unlike its Welsh classmates, it spent its initial years working around Birmingham on suburban passenger services, only later moving to South Wales, and the Swansea and Radyr areas. In 1979 it was purchased by a GWR group based at the Swanage Railway in Dorset, where it has been a regular service locomotive since 2005. Here it is seen in immaculate condition hauling an exhibition freight train at a gala event on the South Devon Railway on 8 April 2009. *Peter Brabham*

The GWR Churchward '45XX' class 2-6-2T small pannier tanks are the archetypal Great Western rural passenger locomotives, once seen all over the GWR network. No 4561 is an example of the highly photogenic initial version with parallel-sided tanks, built in 1924. It was a much-travelled engine, being initially based around Wolverhampton, then spending most of its working life in the West Country before being withdrawn in May 1962. No 4561 was purchased from Barry in 1975 by the then fledgling West Somerset Railway, and was returned to steam in August 1989 after a £100,000 restoration programme, working for nine years until 1998. It is seen here leaving Blue Anchor station on the West Somerset Railway in 1998, just at the end of its certification, since when it was been stored out of use in museums, but in 2011 it was dismantled for a major overhaul.

Peter Brabham

ABOVE **GWR 'Small Prairie' No 4588
has the extended sloping side tanks
for extra water capacity. Built in
1927, it was again a much-travelled
locomotive on the Great Western
network, working initially in the West
Midlands but eventually moving to
Plymouth until withdrawal in 1962.
It was purchased from Barry in 1970
for use on the Dart Valley Railway
in Devon, but had the distinction
of being restored on contract at BR's
Swindon Works. Since 1971 it has
seen work on the South Devon and
Paignton & Dartmouth Railways, and
here makes a fine sight descending
the bank from Churston towards
Paignton, hauling tourists on a sunny
day in August 1993.** *Peter Brabham*

LEFT **GWR 'Small Prairie' No 4566, built
in 1924, was the eighth locomotive to
be purchased from Barry scrapyard,
in 1970, and the first of many to find
a home on the Severn Valley Railway.
Having spent all its working life in
the West Country, No 4566 was finally
withdrawn in April 1962. Towed out
of Barry on a freight train in August
1970, it has been a regular on the SVR
since steaming again in July 1975.
Here it makes a rare appearance on
the Gwili Railway in West Wales in
August 1994.** *Peter Brabham*

'Small Prairie' No 5521 spent virtually all its working life between 1927 and 1962 in the West Country. It was purchased from Barry in 1975 for the West Somerset Railway, but then moved to the Dean Forest Railway. Restoration did not commence until the mid-2000s, when it was fully restored at the Flour Mill workshops in the Forest of Dean by 2006. It then went on an amazing tour of Eastern Europe, through Poland and Hungary, at one point heading the 'Venice-Simplon Orient Express' – quite a story for a lowly Great Western tank engine! Here No 5521 is seen on 4 May 2010 at Didcot, just back from its European travels. *Peter Brabham*

GWR 'Prairie' No 5541 covered more than a million miles during its 34-year working life in Cornwall and Somerset, and in north-west Wales on the Cambrian lines, before withdrawal in 1962. It was purchased from Barry in 1972 for use on the Dean Forest Railway, and its intact condition meant that it was able to be returned to steam in just three years. Its 36-year life on the Dean Forest line has required three major overhauls, and it is presently undergoing another restoration. It is seen near Lydney under the autumnal trees of 1998.

Peter Brabham

RIGHT GWR 'Small Prairie' No 5542 is another locomotive that travelled greatly during its working life, from Gloucestershire to Cornwall, until its final withdrawal in 1962. It was purchased in 1975 from Barry scrapyard for the West Somerset Railway, but was not returned to steam until 2002. Here it is seen running along the River Dart on the South Devon Railway on 8 April 2009.

Peter Brabham

LEFT GWR 'Small Prairie' No 5526 was a West Country-based locomotive through its working life from 1928 to 1962. It spent 22 years in Barry scrapyard, during which time most of its parts were stripped for spares for sister locomotives. No 5526 was privately purchased in 1985, first moving to Gloucestershire, then Swindon, and eventually finding a home at the South Devon Railway, where it had been returned to steam by 2008. It is seen here in plain BR black livery at a gala event at Buckfastleigh station on 8 April 2009.

Peter Brabham

ABOVE In 1986, GWR No 5552 became the 174th locomotive to leave Barry, after 26 years in the salty sea air. The sad remains of the locomotive were purchased for eventual use on the Bodmin & Wenford Railway, which meant going home to its last working region of Plymouth. After a major restoration programme, No 5552 returned to steam in August 2003 and is seen here at Totnes Riverside, on hire to the South Devon Railway for a GWR gala on 8 April 2009. *Peter Brabham*

RIGHT GWR 'Small Prairie' No 5572 was the 15th locomotive to leave Barry, back in 1971, when the Great Western Society could take its pick of the best 'Prairie' tanks on offer in the scrapyard. The locomotive initially moved to the Taunton Branch of the GWS, but later went on to the Didcot base, where it is seen working in 1986. Since returning to steam in 1985, No 5572 has worked on heritage lines such as the West Somerset. It has been out of boiler certification for many years and is now just a static exhibit at the Didcot museum. *Peter Brabham*

ABOVE **When you look at an immaculate GWR 'Small Prairie' No 5553 shunting at Washford station on the West Somerset Railway, it is hard to believe that it is the same locomotive as the wreck that spent 28 years and 2 months in Woodham Brothers' scrapyard, as seen in earlier chapters of this book. No 5553 was the 213th and last locomotive to leave Barry, in January 1990, and holds the record for having spent the longest time in the scrapyard. The financial resources of pop music maestro Pete Waterman were brought to bear on the locomotive's professional restoration by Tyseley Museum, Birmingham. Like all its sister locomotives, during its working life between 1928 and 1961 No 5553 was allocated all over the Great Western system from Bristol to Pwllheli and as far as St Blazey in Cornwall.** Peter Brabham

RIGHT **A double-heading pair of ex-Barry scrapyard GWR Prairie locomotives, Nos 5553 and 5521 are seen leaving Crowcombe Heathfield station on the West Somerset Railway in April 2007.** *Peter Brabham*

ABOVE The Great Western 2-6-2T 'Large Prairies' of the Collett '5101' class were built with larger driving wheels for use on fast passenger work all over the GWR system. No 4141 was built in 1946 and worked around the Gloucester area until withdrawal in 1963. It was purchased in 1973 and towed by rail, together with three other locomotives, to the Severn Valley Railway. Since restoration, No 4141 has worked on the Great Central and Llangollen Railways, and is seen here on shed at the Gloucestershire Warwickshire Railway in May 2006. In 2012 No 4141 completed a major overhaul at Llangollen for its future use on the Epping Ongar Railway in Essex. *Peter Brabham*

LEFT Collett 'Large Prairie' No 4144 was purchased from Barry scrapyard in 1974 by the Great Western Society, Didcot, as its representative of this class. Built in 1946, No 4144 carried out a variety of duties in Wales, from banking trains through the Severn Tunnel to hauling passenger trains deep in the Welsh coalfield valleys. It is seen here working on the exhibition line at the Didcot centre in August 2005. *Peter Brabham*

'Large Prairie' No 4160 was built in 1948 and allocated to Barry shed, from where it hauled local passenger services until 1965. It departed from Barry in 1974, first for Tyseley then later to the Plym Valley Railway in Plymouth. Finally the disassembled parts moved to the West Somerset Railway in 1990 for restoration.

No 4160 first hauled a passenger train again on 6 August 1993, and is now a regular service locomotive on the WSR, where it is seen awaiting its turn on shed at Minehead. *Peter Brabham*

ABOVE GWR No 5164 was the 30th locomotive to leave Barry, in 1973, moving to the Severn Valley Railway, where it was back home, as during its working life from 1930 to 1963 it had been based largely in the Wolverhampton area. Due to the intact nature of the locomotive back in 1973, it was restored to steam by 1979. During more than 30 years of service on the SVR, No 5164 has required regular major overhauls. The locomotive is seen here at Bewdley during an SVR autumn gala event in September 2009.
Peter Brabham

LEFT GWR 'Large Prairie' No 5199, built in 1934, was withdrawn from service in 1963 after working mainly in the West Midlands. It spent 22 years in the scrapyard until it was purchased for preservation in 1985. A long restoration programme commenced at a number of bases until it was finally restored at Long Marston, steaming again in 2003. No 5199 has visited many heritage railways and its seen here at the Gloucestershire Warwickshire Railway in April 2004. In the spring of 2012, the locomotive was outshopped in plain black livery on the Llangollen Railway with another 10-year boiler certificate.
Peter Brabham

ABOVE The large Great Western '42XX' class 2-8-0 tanks were designed for heavy short-distance freight work, their primary duties being on South Wales coal traffic and the china clay trains of Cornwall. No 4247 carried out both the South Wales and Cornish duties during its working life from 1916 to 1964. In 1985 it was purchased and restored on the Gloucestershire Warwickshire Railway, where it is seen at Toddington in March 2005. It is now a regular service engine on the Bodmin & Wenford Railway in Cornwall. *Peter Brabham*

RIGHT GWR No 4248 was purchased from Barry scrapyard in 1986 for use in a diorama at the STEAM museum at Swindon Works, depicting the role of women employed in the works during the Second World War. The 2-8-0 tank locomotive is largely unrecognisable stripped right down to its frames and boiler. *Peter Brabham*

ABOVE In total contrast to the previous locomotive, sister engine No 4277 is restored and painted in full GWR lined passenger livery and named *Hercules* on the Paignton & Dartmouth Railway, a long way from its mundane working life from 1920 to 1964 on South Wales coal traffic. Here No 4277 is seen attacking the steep bank at Goodrington on 2 August 2010. It was privately purchased in 1986 and restored to working order by 1996. The locomotive was subsequently sold on to the Paignton & Dartmouth Railway in 2008, where it is now a regular service engine. *Peter Brabham*

LEFT GWR No 5224 is another heavy freight locomotive, and spent its working life from 1924 to 1963 around Newport and Cardiff. In 1978 it departed from Barry scrapyard for the Great Central Railway at Loughborough, returning to steam in 1984. Here the locomotive is seen at Toddington, on loan to the Gloucestershire Warwickshire Railway in September 2004. *Peter Brabham*

Not for the purists, but GWR No 5239 looks absolutely splendid with its lined passenger livery and *Goliath* nameplate here at Brunel's Kingswear station on 3 August 2010. Most tourists travelling on the Paignton & Dartmouth Railway would not believe that No 5239 was a mundane South Wales heavy freight locomotive. Built in 1924, it was withdrawn in 1963 and purchased ten years later for use on the Devonian tourist railway.
Peter Brabham

No 5322 is one of only two Great Western 2-6-0 tender locomotives to end up in Barry scrapyard, and has an interesting history. Built in 1917 during the First World War, it was shipped off to France under the control of the Railway Operating Division (ROD) of the Army. Returning to the UK in 1919, it became a regular GWR locomotive, working all over the network until final withdrawal in 1964. No 5322 spent only four years in the scrapyard before being purchased by the Great Western Society. Initially restored by the Caerphilly branch of the society, No 5322 was subsequently moved to the Didcot centre. It is seen here on the Gloucestershire Warwickshire Railway in May 2010 in its ROD livery.
Peter Brabham

No 7325 is the other 2-6-0 tender locomotive that found its way to Barry scrapyard. It was initially numbered by the GWR as 9303, which often causes some confusion in scrapyard images. Built in 1932, it worked all over the GWR system, ending up at Pontypool in 1964, and was then sent for scrap to Barry. It was purchased in 1974 by the Great Western (SVR) Association, but did not return to steam until 1992. No 7325 is seen here in September 1993 on shed at Bridgnorth. During the late 1990s it was main-line certified, working charter trains double-headed with other locomotives. *Peter Brabham*

ABOVE No 3802 is an example of the younger Collett version of the GWR '28XX' class, built in 1938. The locomotive spent much of its working life hauling long-distance iron-ore trains from the Banbury orefields to the South Wales steelworks until withdrawal in 1965. Privately purchased in 1984, it had been restored to steam on the Llangollen Railway by mid-2005. Here No 3802 is seen working at a West Somerset autumn gala in September 2007. *Peter Brabham*

LEFT The Churchward '28XX' class and Collett '2884' class 2-8-0 tender locomotives were the long-distance heavy freight locomotives of the Great Western Railway. Fifteen of them ended up in Barry scrapyard, and have not proved to be very popular as restoration projects. Here No 2807 is seen leaving Cheltenham Racecourse station on the Gloucestershire Warwickshire Railway in April 2011. The locomotive was built in 1905 (the oldest locomotive in Barry scrapyard) and withdrawn in 1963. Purchased in 1981, its restoration took 29 years, completed on the Gloucestershire Warwickshire Railway in 2010. *Peter Brabham*

TOP Built in 1918, GWR heavy freight 2-8-0 No 2857 was withdrawn in 1963 after working all over the Great Western network on freight duties. In 1975 it was the first of the '28XX' class to be purchased from Barry, by a group of Severn Valley Railway members, for £5,775; this took a three-year appeal for funds, the asking price having started out in 1972 at £3,500. No 2857 was assessed as being in the best mechanical condition of the 15 of this type in the scrapyard, and moved by rail to the SVR in August 1975, together with No 7325. No 2857 returned to steam in September 1979, but had cylinder problems. Amazingly, in the demolition of Briton Ferry steelworks in 1979 a set of scrapped '28XX' cylinders was uncovered and used in a repair completed by 1984. No 2857 is seen here on loan to the Gloucestershire Warwickshire Railway in 1992. It has the distinction of hauling a demonstration historical freight train to Newport station on the main line on 10 September 1985. It ran out of boiler certification on the SVR in December 1994, but returned to steam there in August 2011 with another ten-year certificate. *Peter Brabham*

ABOVE No 3803 was built in 1939 and withdrawn from Severn Tunnel Junction in 1963. It was purchased from Barry in 1983 for use on the South Devon Railway; restoration was carried out at Tyseley, and it returned to steam on the South Devon line in 2006. No 3803 is now resident at the Gloucestershire Warwickshire Railway, where it is seen at a gala in May 2010.
Peter Brabham

RIGHT GWR No 3822 was purchased by the Great Western Society in 1976 as its representative of the heavy freight locomotives. It has been out on loan to various preservation lines, but it is seen here at Didcot in May 2010.
Peter Brabham

TOP GWR No 3850 was bought from Barry in 1984 for restoration and use on the West Somerset Railway. It returned to steam in 2005 and can be seen regularly hauling passenger trains on the Somerset heritage railway line. It is pictured here running round at Minehead station on the WSR during the 2012 Spring Gala event. *Peter Brabham*

ABOVE The Great Western 4-6-0 'Manor' class are ideal locomotives for the longer heritage lines as they were designed for lighter-weight rural cross-country lines, especially in Mid Wales. No 7802 *Bradley Manor* is seen here entering Bewdley on the Severn Valley Railway in March 2010. The locomotive was initially purchased from Barry in 1979 as a source of spares for sister locomotive No 7812. However, it was later decided to restore *Bradley Manor* on the SVR, which was achieved in 1993. *Peter Brabham*

FACING PAGE TOP **No 7812 *Erlestoke Manor* was purchased from Barry in 1974 and moved initially to Ashchurch, then to the Severn Valley Railway by 1976. It was quickly restored by September 1979 and was a regular service engine on the SVR throughout the 1980s. Having spent a long time subsequently out of service, No 7812 was recently overhauled again and it seen working at Bewdley on the SVR in March 2010.** *Peter Brabham*

FACING PAGE BOTTOM **GWR No 7819 *Hinton Manor* is another 'Manor' class locomotive based on the Severn Valley Railway, where it is seen in 1993 at Bewdley painted in BR lined black livery. Purchased in 1973 from Barry scrapyard, No 7819 was returned to steam by June 1977. During the mid-1980s it was main-line certified and ran over the steep Devon banks double-heading with other GWR locomotives. It has been out of certification for many years and spent a period as the café exhibit at Swindon Shopping Centre. A new fundraising campaign is under way to restore the locomotive again for work on the Severn Valley Railway.** *Peter Brabham*

THIS PAGE TOP **GWR No 7820 *Dinmore Manor* is one of the West Somerset Railway's examples of this locomotive class. Purchased in 1979 and originally intended for the Gwili Railway, the unrestored locomotive was re-sold in 1984 and moved to the West Somerset Railway. Restoration was contracted out to Tyseley, and the locomotive was working on the WSR by September 1995. After a decade of regular activity on the Somerset heritage line, No 7820 is now out of boiler certification and money is being raised for another major overhaul. The locomotive is seen here in 1996 pulling out of Bishops Lydeard station on the WSR.** *Peter Brabham*

RIGHT **GWR No 7822 *Foxcote Manor* left Barry in 1975 for North Wales, based initially at Oswestry, then the Llangollen Railway, where it is now resident. Returned to steam in 1987, No 7822 became a regular service engine on the line. In 2010 it underwent another major overhaul and has another 10 years of boiler certification. *Foxcote Manor* is seen here in April 2011 pulling out of Llangollen.** *Peter Brabham*

TOP GWR No 7827 *Lydham Manor* was the first of the eight 'Manor' locomotives to leave Barry scrapyard, in June 1970, being only the fifth locomotive to leave. Originally intended for the South Devon Railway, No 7827 was restored by April 1973 and has spent all its preserved life working on the Paignton & Dartmouth line hauling tourist trains. It is seen here on its only excursion away from the South Devon line, at the Didcot GWR 175th anniversary gala on 4 May 2010. *Peter Brabham*

ABOVE No 7828 *Odney Manor* did not leave Barry until 1981 for the Gloucestershire Warwickshire Railway, returning to steam by 1987. The restoration cost £87,750, without including many hundreds of hours of unpaid labour costs. It has been seen working on many preserved lines, the most unlikely being the East Lancashire Railway, where the 'Manor' is pictured at Ramsbottom in April 1993. In September 2011 No 7828 returned to steam on the West Somerset Railway renamed as Norton Manor. *Peter Brabham*

TOP The final restored GWR 'Manor', No 7821 *Ditcheat Manor*, is seen here in 1998 at a West Somerset gala event sandwiched between Nos 7820 *Dinmore Manor* and 7828 *Odney Manor*. No 7821 was purchased from Barry scrapyard in 1981 and restored at Llangollen. Since 1998 it has worked mainly on the Great Central Railway at Loughborough, and was then stored at the Cambrian Railway at Oswestry. In July 2008, No 7821 was purchased by the West Somerset Railway, but is presently on static display in the STEAM museum at Swindon. *Peter Brabham*

ABOVE The 'Hall' class were the hard-working mixed-traffic locomotives of the Great Western Railway, and 17 of them ended up in Barry scrapyard. Here No 4920 *Dumbleton Hall* is observed at Toddington in 1996 working on the Gloucestershire Warwickshire Railway. No 4920 left Barry in 1976 and was restored on the South Devon Railway by 1990. Being too heavy for the small GWR branch line, the locomotive operated principally on the Paignton & Dartmouth Railway until 2000, since when it has been stored out of service at Buckfastleigh. *Peter Brabham*

LEFT In July 1985, Nos 4930 *Hagley Hall* and 7819 *Hinton Manor* attack the steep Dainton bank on the Great Western main line in Devon, part of the GWR 150th anniversary celebrations. No 4930 left Barry in 1973 for restoration on the Severn Valley Railway, returning to steam on the main line in September 1979. A high-profile main-line certified engine during the 1980s, No 4930 has been out of service on the SVR for more than a decade. *Peter Brabham*

RIGHT GWR No 4936 *Kinlet Hall* did not leave Barry until 1981, after 16 years in the scrapyard. It moved around various restoration centres until returning to steam in 2000. Here *Kinlet Hall* powers away from a signal check at Doniford during a West Somerset Railway spring gala on 30 March 2009. *Peter Brabham*

FACING PAGE TOP GWR No 4953 *Pitchford Hall* was a late Barry restoration project, leaving the scrapyard only in 1984. Privately purchased by Dr John Kennedy, the locomotive returned to steam in February 2004 after an extensive rebuild at Tyseley costing nearly £1 million. No 4953 was certified a year later for main-line running, which it usually did in tandem with *Rood Ashton Hall*. Here No 4953 is seen hauling a freight train though the picturesque Carrog station during a Llangollen Railway gala event on 13 September 2010. In the spring of 2012, seven years into its ten-year boiler certification, the locomotive was purchased by Mr Roger Wright for use on his Epping Ongar heritage railway in Essex. *Peter Brabham*

FACING PAGE BOTTOM Throughout its time in Barry scrapyard GWR No 4965 *Rood Ashton Hall* was always known as No 4983 *Albert Hall*, but after purchase in 1970 the subsequent restoration revealed its true identity. No 4983 was the first 'Hall' to leave Barry, in 1970, to be restored at Tyseley Museum. However, it took 31 years to restore the locomotive, completed in 2001. Over the past decade No 4965 has been a regular main-line certified engine, and is seen here with GWR 'Castle' No 5043 on a main-line special at Didcot station on 2 April 2011. *Peter Brabham*

THIS PAGE TOP 5900 *Hinderton Hall* was the 14th locomotive to leave Barry scrapyard in 1971 bound for the Great Western Society at Didcot. Five years later in 1976, after a major overhaul 5900 was returned to steam. Mainline *certified during the late 1970s, Hinderton Hall* saw extensive mainline use on charter trains. Now out of boiler certification, 5900 is captured on display as a static exhibit outside Didcot depot in May 2010. *Peter Brabham*

RIGHT No 6960 *Raveningham Hall* was an early restoration project, leaving Barry in 1972. Privately owned, it moved to Steamtown, Carnforth, for restoration. In 1975 it made an appearance at the Rail 150 event at Shildon, Co Durham, and also took part in the Swansea-Carmarthen GWR 150 events in West Wales in 1985. Then followed periods of work on the Severn Valley (from 1977) and the Gloucestershire Warwickshire Railway, as seen here in 1995. Now one of a fleet of steam engines owned by millionaire investment banker Jeremy Hosking, *Raveningham Hall* came to the end of a major overhaul on the West Somerset Railway in 2011 and should return to steam in 2012. *Peter Brabham*

TOP No 6990 *Witherslack Hall* was purchased in 1975 and moved from Barry to the Great Central Railway at Loughborough. It was a regular service engine on the GCR after returning to steam in 1986 in BR lined black livery, and is seen here on loan at the Gloucestershire Warwickshire Railway in May 1997. It is presently out of boiler certification. *Peter Brabham*

ABOVE No 7903 *Foremarke Hall* is one of two examples of the younger Hawksworth 'Hall' locomotives built in 1949-50 by British Railways that ended up in Barry scrapyard. No 7903 did not leave until 1981, bound for the Swindon & Cricklade Railway. Returning to steam in 2004, it is normally found on the Gloucestershire Warwickshire Railway, where it was photographed hauling a freight train at Toddington on 24 May 2009. *Peter Brabham*

ABOVE GWR No 5972 *Olton Hall* is another Great Western 'Hall' locomotive that was withdrawn in 1963 and bought by Dai Woodham for scrap. In 1981 it was purchased privately and partially restored in Wakefield before moving to Carnforth for completion. Around 1999 the first 'Harry Potter' film was being planned and the producers were looking for a suitable steam engine that looked old enough for filming the King's Cross and Scottish scenes. The rest is history – No 5972 was chosen, painted crimson and named *Hogwarts Castle*. Eight films later it is a film star, and has replaced No 71000 as the most famous Barry scrapyard locomotive. It also has a twin, built for the 'Harry Potter' theme park in the USA. When not filming, No 5972 normally carries the *Olton Hall* nameplates, but here in June 2009 it is seen at the Gloucestershire Warwickshire Railway special 'Harry Potter' event in its *Hogwarts Castle* guise. *Peter Brabham*

ABOVE Only five of the 171 magnificent Great Western 'Castle' class locomotives ended up as scrap in Barry, and four of them have been returned to working order. Here No 5029 *Nunney Castle* is seen on shed at the Great Western Society at Didcot in May 2010. No 5029 was privately purchased from Barry in 1976 for the GWS, the last 'Castle' to leave the yard. Main-line certified and now privately owned by Jeremy Hosking, No 5029 is often seen hauling main-line specials around the UK. *Peter Brabham*

FACING PAGE TOP No 5043 *Earl of Mount Edgcumbe* was withdrawn from service in 1963, bought by Woodham's for scrap in 1964, and re-sold in 1973 to the Birmingham Railway Museum, Tyseley. The locomotive lay unrestored for more than 20 years before finally returning to steam in 2008 with main-line certification. It is hard to believe when you look at the magnificence of the engine, seen here in April 2011 at Didcot, that it was out of action for 45 years. No 5043 is based at Tyseley, and can be seen regularly hauling Birmingham to Stratford-upon-Avon tourist trains. *Peter Brabham*

FACING PAGE BOTTOM No 5080 *Defiant* was named after the Second World War aeroplane, having originally been named *Ogmore Castle*. It was withdrawn from traffic in 1963 and sold for scrap to Woodham's at Barry. No 5080 was purchased from Barry in 1974 and moved by rail to Birmingham Railway Museum, Tyseley. By 1988 it had been restored with main-line certification and pulled a number of main-line specials as well as visiting heritage lines for a decade. Here No 5080 is pictured on such a main-line special on 16 April 1990, standing at Stratford-upon-Avon station. Now out of boiler certification, *Defiant* can be seen as a static exhibit at the Buckinghamshire Railway Museum at Quainton Road. *Peter Brabham*

ABOVE This magnificent train was part of the GWR 150 celebrations on Sunday 7 July 1985. GWR 'Castle' No 5051 *Drysllwyn Castle* and 'Hall' No 4930 *Hagley Hall* pull the 'Great Western Limited' out of Bristol Temple Meads to Plymouth. No 5051 was the fourth locomotive and first 'Castle' class out of Barry scrapyard, in 1970. Restored to steam at the Great Western Society Didcot by 1980, it has been a main-line certified engine ever since. As No 5051 carried two names as a Great Western engine, it is presently named in its other guise as *Earl Bathurst*, which often causes confusion. However, all is not as rosy as it seems in this picture, as the engines failed to get past the steep Devon banks and the train terminated at Totnes. On close inspection, a third Barry locomotive can be seen, No 6023 *King Edward II*, in the fish dock. This was the first restoration base for the 'King' before moving to Didcot for its long-awaited return to steam in 2011. *Peter Brabham*

ABOVE No 6024 *King Edward I* leaves Paddington station on a frosty winter morning in February 1992 – it doesn't get better than this! No 6024 was much the better example of the two 'King' class locomotives found in Barry scrapyard in 1973. Sold to the King Preservation Society and moved to the Buckinghamshire Railway Museum, Quainton Road, a long restoration to main-line certification took place, the locomotive returning to steam in 1989. Over the past 20 years it has been a regular main-line performer, while also visiting numerous heritage lines. Internal politics and court cases between members of the society resulted in the sale of the locomotive in December 2010 to a trust. In 2012 the ten-year boiler certificate expired and another major overhaul was required. *Peter Brabham*

LEFT To any GWR enthusiast, the only sight better than a 'Castle' locomotive is two coupled together running on the main line. 'Castles' Nos 5043 *Earl of Mount Edgcumbe* and 5029 *Nunney Castle* approach Newport, Monmouthshire, in May 2009. *Peter Brabham*

RIGHT As well documented in previous chapters of this book, No 6023 *King Edward II* was in a terrible condition back in 1984 at Barry scrapyard. Stripped of nearly all parts, and with a cut driving wheel, the second 'King' was in serious danger of being cut up. It was originally purchased from Woodham's for £12,000, but Harvey's of Bristol re-purchased the locomotive for £22,000 and moved it to Temple Meads station in 1984. After the stalling of that venture, No 6023 was re-sold to the Great Western Society at Didcot. Twenty-seven years later, on 2 April 2011, it is seen cutting the yellow ribbon marking its official re-launch at Didcot – a magnificent dedicated effort of heritage preservation. *Peter Brabham*

ABOVE On 28 April 2011, No 6023 *King Edward II* was joined by No 6024 *King Edward I* at the Didcot centre. Here the GWR 'super-power' pair haul a two-coach train on the exhibition line. No 6023 spent the summer months of 2011 running in on the Mid-Norfolk Railway, but this proved troublesome with the 'King' experiencing boiler problems. It was stripped down again for more than eight months to resolve the technical issues, sadly delaying its planned use on mainline excursions in the autumn of 2011, in tandem with its Barry sister No 6024.
David Brabham

RIGHT That day provided a sight that many people thought they would never see in their lifetime – No 6024 *King Edward I* in full British Railways blue livery working again at Didcot, 49 years after it was sold for scrap to Barry scrapyard.
Peter Brabham

6

Southern Railway steam locomotives purchased from Barry scrapyard

In total, 41 former Southern Railway locomotives were purchased from Barry scrapyard, and the types and numbers are listed below. Those numbers in **bold** are locomotives that have been returned to steam, but may currently be in store out of boiler certification or under overhaul.

0-6-0 tender locomotives
30541

2-6-0 tender locomotives
31618 31625 31638 31806 31874

4-6-0 tender locomotives
30499 **30506** 30825 **30828** 30830 **30841 30847**

4-6-2 'West Country'/'Battle of Britain' class
34007 34010 **34016 34027 34028 34039 34046 34053** 34058 **34059 34067 34070 34072** 34073 **34081 34092 34101 34105**

4-6-2 'Merchant Navy' class
35005 35006 35009 35010 35011 35018 35022 **35025 35027** 35029

The preservation of Southern Railway locos is in the main due to the formation in 1960 of the Bluebell Railway, followed by the Kent & East Sussex and Isle of Wight lines, where a selection of historically significant locos found a home after being purchased direct from British Railways. In addition, there are a number of important locos in the National Collection at York, representing the 'Schools', 'King Arthur', 'Lord Nelson', 'Q1', 'M7', 'T9', Beattie well tanks and 19th-century classes that did not end up at Barry.

One remarkable aspect of the Barry record is that 28 Bulleid 'Pacifics' were in the scrapyard. This is due to the fact that the whole class was withdrawn in the 1965-67 period, the exact time window when Woodham's was buying locos. Also, as South Wales scrapyards were the geographically nearest for the Southern locos, more than half the class were scrapped in South Wales. Without these 28 locos as part of the heritage railway and main-line pool, only three Bulleid 'Pacifics' would have been preserved, and no examples of the rebuilt 'light Pacifics'. Those three would have been Nos 34023 *Blackmore Vale*, 34051 *Winston Churchill* (part of the National Collection), and 35026 *Clan Line*.

One future construction project might be to 'unrebuild' a 'Merchant Navy' locomotive back to its original condition with chain drive and 'air-smoothed' casing. In 2006 it was proposed that unrestored No 35018 *British India Line* could be used for such a project, but the idea has now been dropped due to the costs involved.

FACING PAGE TOP Southern Railway Maunsell 'Q' Class 0-6-0 No 541 (BR 30541) is the only survivor of this class of 20 locomotives in preservation. The locomotive was purchased by a preservation group in 1973, and originally moved to Gloucestershire; it is now one of five locomotives owned by the Maunsell Locomotive Society. No 541 was restored to steam on the Bluebell Railway in November 1983 and is seen here in December 1991 on a works train at Vaux End Bridge, re-laying the extension to Sharpthorne. The locomotive is now out of boiler certification, but returned to the Bluebell Railway workshops in 2012 with the aim of working again in 2013. *Barry Smith (Maunsell Locomotive Society)*

FACING PAGE BOTTOM SR No 506 (BR 30506) is a Urie 'S15' class locomotive built in 1920 and withdrawn in 1964 after accumulating 1,227,897 miles in 43 years. The locomotive moved to Barry under its own steam, and was purchased in 1973 for £4,000, just before VAT was introduced. It moved to the then embryonic Mid Hants Railway in 1976. Preservation was halted by the poor state of the boiler, so that of sister locomotive No 30825 at Barry was swapped in 1981. The locomotive returned to steam in 1987 and is seen here in full Southern livery on the line. *Peter Brabham*

LEFT Maunsell 'S15' class 4-6-0 No 30828, in Southern livery as No 828, pulls away from Yeovil Junction station on 8 October 1994. No 30828 was withdrawn from service in Salisbury in 1964 with a final mileage of 1,287,124. It left Barry in 1981 and was restored by the Eastleigh Railway Preservation Society at Eastleigh, Hampshire, with financial help from Eastleigh Council. Restoration was completed by 1993, and No 828 was named *Harry A. Frith* in 1996. The locomotive was certified to main-line standard, including runs over the Settle & Carlisle and visits to the East Somerset and Swanage heritage railways. Its boiler certification expired in 2002 and No 828 is now undergoing a second major overhaul at the Mid Hants Railway. *John Wiltshire*

BELOW SR No 1618 (BR 31618) is a Maunsell 'U' class 2-6-0 locomotive scrapped in 1964. In 1969 it became the second locomotive to be purchased out of Barry, by the Southern Mogul Preservation Society for £2,000, and was taken to New Hythe, Kent, in 1969. It was then moved to the Kent & East Sussex Railway for restoration, but was too heavy to run there. In 1977 it moved to the Bluebell Railway, where it has been a regular service engine over the past 30 years, as seen here at Sheffield Park station in May 1992. *Peter Brabham*

SR No 30841 is a Maunsell 'S15' class locomotive withdrawn from service in 1964. Purchased from Barry in 1974, it was restored in Essex and named *Greene King* after the brewery; it was main-line certified in the late 1970s. In 1986 the remaining frames of sister locomotive No 30825 were purchased from Barry and used for restoration, so to add confusion the locomotive presently runs with this alternative number, as convention dictates that the number of an engine is determined by its frames, not its boiler. Since 1978, No 30841/30825 has been a regular performer on the North Yorkshire Moors Railway, where it is seen in March 1992. *Peter Brabham*

TOP Maunsell 'U' class 2-6-0 No 31625 stands on Ropley shed on the Mid Hants Railway in April 1998. Built in 1929, the locomotive was converted to oil-firing as an experiment in 1947, but converted back to coal a year later. Withdrawn from Guildford in 1964, it was privately purchased from Woodham Brothers in 1980 for use on the Mid Hants Railway. In 1999 the locomotive took part in the 'Steam on the Met' events on London Underground's Metropolitan Line between Harrow-on-the-Hill and Watford. *Andrew Wiltshire*

ABOVE No 31806 is another Maunsell 'U' class locomotive, built in 1926 and sent for scrap in 1964. When built it was a 'K' class 2-6-4 tank engine named *River Torridge*, but after a major derailment disaster at Sevenoaks with a classmate, it was rebuilt in 1928 as a tender locomotive. Withdrawn in 1964 and stored at Fratton, it arrived at Barry in 1964 together with No 31625. Privately purchased by John Bunch in 1975, it moved out of Barry the following year for use on the then planned Mid Hants Railway. Restoration took only three years, from 1979 to April 1981. No 31806 was a regular Mid Hants service engine for a decade, as seen here in 1986. Out of boiler certification for many years, it returned again to work on the line in 2011 after a major overhaul. *Peter Brabham*

TOP No 31874 is the only example of the 50 Maunsell 'N' class locomotives in preservation. It was one of 100 built in 1923 in kit form as a post-First World War Woolwich Arsenal initiative for sale at £4,000 each. It was purchased by the Southern Railway and assembled at Ashford as No A874. After covering 966,499 miles in service it was withdrawn from the West Country in 1964 and sold to Woodham Brothers for scrap. No 31874 was purchased from Barry by John Bunch in 1974 and was rapidly restored on the Mid Hants Railway by April 1977. Originally named *Aznar Line* after a financial sponsor, the locomotive is seen here in 1989 carrying the name *Brian Fisk*, who at the time was the proprietor of *Mayfair* magazine and contributed substantially to the cost of restoration, which was completed entirely outdoors. No 31874 was a Mid Hants mainstay locomotive in the late 1970s and 1980s, but is presently out of boiler certification on that line. *Peter Brabham*

ABOVE No 31874 is seen again minus smoke deflectors in its Rev Awdry's 'James the Red Engine' guise on shed at Ropley on the Mid Hants Railway in September 1994. *John Wiltshire*

FACING PAGE TOP No 34007 *Wadebridge* is the oldest of the 18 Bulleid 'West Country'/'Battle of Britain' class locomotives sent to Barry for scrap between 1963 and 1965. It is also an example of the original Bulleid design with the characteristic 'air-smoothed' casing. No 34007 was purchased in 1981 for restoration at the Plym Valley Railway, later moving to the Bodmin & Wenford Railway. Returning to steam on the line in 2005, it has since been moved to the Mid Hants Railway, where it is a regular service locomotive. The locomotive is seen here on loan at the Gloucestershire Warwickshire Railway in July 2009. *Peter Brabham*

FACING PAGE BOTTOM 'West Country' class No 34016 *Bodmin* was built in 1945, and rebuilt in 1958. *Bodmin* was the second Bulleid Pacific to be purchased privately from Barry, in 1972. Originally moving to Buckinghamshire, the locomotive had relocated to the rapidly developing Mid Hants Railway by 1976.

A short three-year restoration brought the locomotive back to working order by 1979. A regular service locomotive on the line for many years, as seen above in 1998, it is presently out of boiler certification. *Peter Brabham*

THIS PAGE TOP No 34027 *Taw Valley* is a rebuilt 'West Country' class locomotive. Purchased in 1980, restoration commenced in the North of England but was completed on the Severn Valley Railway in 1989. A regular main-line certified engine, it is seen here in July 1996 on Didcot shed. *Taw Valley* is presently undergoing another major overhaul at Bridgnorth shed on the SVR. *Peter Brabham*

THIS PAGE BOTTOM Rebuilt Bulleid Pacific No 34028 *Eddystone* did not leave Barry until 1986 and was initially restored at a private site in Kent. It has been operating on the Swanage Railway since 2004, as caught here in the setting sun at Swanage station on 12 September 2008. *Peter Brabham*

FACING PAGE TOP No 34039 *Boscastle* left Barry in 1973 after being privately purchased for £3,250 by James Tawse as a family restoration project, later widening to become the Boscastle Locomotive Syndicate to raise the restoration costs. No 34039 was finally restored to steam in November 1992 after a 19-year restoration at the Great Central Railway, Loughborough. *Boscastle* is presently out of boiler certification and in store, and is seen here in steam on shed at Loughborough in 1996. *Peter Brabham*

FACING PAGE BOTTOM As this book was in preparation in the summer of 2012 the latest ex-Barry locomotive to be restored to steam is rebuilt Bulleid 'Battle of Britain' Pacific No 34053 *Sir Keith Park* (named after the famous Air Vice Marshall and hero of both World Wars). In 1979 the remains of No 34053 with a tender from No 35006 were privately purchased by Mr Charles Timms, however it was not until 1984 that the locomotive was moved from Barry to Hull where some initial restoration was carried out. After the death of the owner in 1992, *Sir Keith Park* was sold on to Dr J. F. Kennedy and first moved to Crewe and then onto Chippenham, the tender was sold separately to another restoration project. In 1997 the locomotive was sold on again to Jeremy Hosking who used it as a donor of parts for his other Bullied Pacific, No 34046 *Braunton*, which was under restoration on the West Somerset Railway. In 2000 after picking the best components of the two locomotives for the restoration of *Braunton*, the now

skeletal remains of No 34053 were purchased by Southern Locomotives Ltd and moved to Sellindge in Kent. Southern Locomotives Ltd own five Bulleid Pacifics (and have also sold on two 'Merchant Navy' pacifics) and after their restoration of *Manston* was completed in 2008, they started working in earnest on No 34053. Parts of the locomotive were restored at three different locations and also included the fabrication of a totally new-build tender. By April 2012 the completed locomotive, now located at Herston works near Swanage, was ready for running in, which initially had been intended for the nearby Swanage Railway. However as the Swanage Railway already had two working ex-Barry Bulleid Pacifics, a deal was agreed with the Severn Valley Railway for a summer period of running in followed by a long period working on the famous heritage line as a service locomotive. Above the locomotive is captured on the 31 August 2012 standing at Bridgnorth station during only its second week in traffic.

ABOVE No 34059 *Sir Archibald Sinclair* is a recent Bulleid Pacifics to return to steam, in 2009. The locomotive was actually purchased and moved out of Barry without a tender for use on the Bluebell Railway as far back as 1979, and is an example of the longevity of some Barry restoration projects, taking three decades to full restoration. As a new steam locomotive in the digital photography age, it has been much photographed (except by me), and I am indebted to Dave Bowles for his splendid photo of the locomotive in action on the Bluebell line. *Dave Bowles*

ABOVE No 34046 *Braunton* was the 207th locomotive to leave Barry, in 1988, initially for a heritage project based in Brighton Works. The locomotive was later sold on to a private buyer with the financial resources to underwrite a full restoration on the West Somerset Railway. On returning to steam in 2008, it suffered from a flaw in a driving axle, and the defective axle had to be swapped with one from unrestored No 35011 *General Steam Navigation*. Here No 34046 is seen leaving Minehead on 4 September 2010, and the following year was being prepared for main-line certification. *Peter Brabham*

RIGHT No 34070 *Manston*, an unrebuilt 'Battle of Britain' locomotive, was purchased by the Manston Locomotive Preservation Society in 1983. It moved to Richborough power station in Kent, then later to Sellindge, where other Bulleids were under restoration. After more than two decades of work, the locomotive returned to steam in 2008. *Manston* is normally based on the Swanage Railway in Dorset, but is seen here passing Highley's Engine House on the Severn Valley Railway on 25 September 2010. *Peter Brabham*

No 34067 *Tangmere* was named after the famous Second World War Battle of Britain airfield. After being privately purchased, the locomotive left Barry in 1981, being restored at a number of preservation centres. *Tangmere* returned to steam on the East Lancashire Railway, and is a regular main-line certified locomotive running mainly around the South East of England. Here the locomotive is seen on a visit to the West Somerset Railway on 24 March 2006.
Peter Brabham

TOP No 34072 *257 Squadron* moved out of Barry in 1984 for restoration on the Swanage Railway. After a decade of running on the Swanage and other heritage lines between 1994 and 2004, the locomotive is now out of certification. It is seen here on 12 April 1997 right at the end of its boiler certification at Swanage, in a glorious grimy condition not normally seen on heritage lines. *Peter Brabham*

ABOVE No 34081 *92 Squadron* was purchased from Barry scrapyard in 1993 by the Battle of Britain Locomotive Preservation Society, and left Barry in November 1996 for the Nene Valley Railway. The locomotive returned to steam in March 1998 at a cost of £150,000 (excluding labour costs), and has been based mainly in the East of England, making occasional visits to other lines. Presently the locomotive is undergoing its second major overhaul on the Nene Valley Railway. *92 Squadron* is seen here approaching Holt on the North Norfolk Railway on 3 April 2005 in early nationalisation British Railways Malachite Green livery with yellow stripes and sunshine lettering. Presently 92 Squadron is under major overhaul with the aim to return to steam in 2013. *Ian Bowskill/Battle of Britain Preservation Society*

TOP 'West Country' No 34105 *Swanage* is in original form. It left Barry in 1978 for the Mid Hants Railway, returning to steam in August 1987 after being restored entirely inside a plastic tent. Here *Swanage* is seen on a beautiful snowy day in December 1990 hauling a 'Santa Special' on the Mid Hants Railway. The locomotive is presently out of certification and in store at Ropley shed. *Now undergoing overhaul.* Peter Brabham

ABOVE BR Southern rebuilt 'West Country' No 34101 Hartland is probably the most photographically elusive of all the preserved Bulleid Pacifics. Hartland left Barry in 1978 after purchase by Richard Shaw, moving to his engineering works in Derby. The locomotive was completed by October 1993 on the Great Central Railway, where it is captured on shed at Loughborough in October 1994. The locomotive moved on to the North Yorkshire Moors Railway in 1995 where it only ran for a few years. After a long period of deterioration standing in a siding, Hartland is now back in the works again under a major overhaul and it is planned to steam again through the North York Moors in 2013. John Wiltshire

FACING PAGE TOP No 34092 *City of Wells* was the first Bulleid Pacific to leave Barry, in 1971, for restoration on the Keighley & Worth Valley Railway, a long way from its Southern Railway origins. *City of Wells* was restored to main-line standard by 1980 and became a legend with photographers in the 1980s with its pyrotechnic displays over the Settle & Carlisle line, where it is seen here leaving Rise Hill Tunnel in April 1984. It carried the smaller low-sided 4,500-gallon tender, making it photographically different from its preserved classmates. Out of boiler certification by 1989, the locomotive has sadly laid out of steam for 30 years. A major mechanical overhaul on the K&WVR has been progressing, and at the time of writing the locomotive is in its eagerly awaited final stage of returning to steam, with the possibility of a return to main-line action. David Brabham

FACING PAGE BOTTOM No 35005 *Canadian Pacific* was the oldest of the ten Bulleid 'Merchant Navy' Pacific locomotives sent for scrap to Barry. These locomotives have not proved too popular as restoration projects due to their large size, weight and running costs; to date, only two Barry 'Merchant Navies' have been restored to working order. After private purchase, No 35005 left Barry in 1973 for Steamtown, Carnforth, but finally returned to steam on the Great Central Railway, where it is seen on 12 October 1991. *Canadian Pacific* moved on to the Mid hants Railway, but is presently in store, out of boiler certification, at eastleigh Works, near Southampton. *Peter Brabham*

ABOVE No 35027 *Port Line* was the second restored 'Merchant Navy' class locomotive from Barry scrapyard, being purchased in January 1982 by the Port Line Locomotive Project for £6,500. During that year the locomotive was boxed in on the Barry scrap line and it took another eight months before it could be released and moved off site. After a long period of work inside the former Swindon Works site by a restoration group totalling 300 people, *Port Line* returned to steam in 1988. It has since seen work on the Bluebell Railway, and is captured here running around at the Norden terminus of the Swanage Railway in July 2002. 'Merchant Navy' locomotives are too large and heavy for many heritage lines, limiting their options of work, and *Port Line* was sold, together with unrestored No 35022 *Holland America Line*, by Southern Locomotives Ltd to millionaire banker Jeremy Hosking as one of his fleet of 12 steam locomotives. *Port Line* is currently undergoing restoration again at the Southall depot site in West London with the objective of being available to haul main-line charter excursions. *Peter Brabham*

FACING PAGE TOP No 35029 *Ellerman Lines* is one Barry scrapyard locomotive with an unusual outcome. In 1974 it was purchased by the National Railway Museum, York, sectioned and put on display as an educational exhibit to explain the internal workings of a steam locomotive. *Peter Brabham*

FACING PAGE BOTTOM This is the first pairing of two Bulleid Pacifics in preservation, Nos 34105 *Swanage* and 34016 *Bodmin* on the Mid Hants Railway in 1989. *Peter Brabham*

ABOVE Here is another Bulleid Pacific pairing of Nos 34007 *Wadebridge* and 34046 *Braunton* on the West Somerset Railway on 5 October 2008. *Peter Brabham*

7

London Midland & Scottish Railway steam locomotives purchased from Barry scrapyard

In total, 35 former LMS locomotives were purchased from Barry scrapyard, and their types and numbers are listed below. Those numbers in **bold** signify locomotives that have been returned to steam, but may currently be in store out of boiler certification or under overhaul.

0-6-0 'Jinty' tank locomotives
47279 47298 47324 47327 47357 47406 47493

2-6-2 tank locomotives
41312 41313

0-6-0 tender locomotives
43924 44123 **44422**

2-6-0 tender locomotives
42765 42859 **42968** 46428 46447 **46512 46521**

4-6-0 'Black Five' tender locomotives
44901 45163 45293 **45337 45379** 45491

4-6-0 'Jubilee' class
45690 45699

2-8-0 8F tender locomotives
48151 48173 **48305 48431** 48518 **48624**

2-8-0 Somerset & Dorset 7F tender locomotives
53808 53809

Eagerly awaited in the next few years is the return to steam of 'Jubilee' class No 45699 *Galatea*. Virtually given up as a lost cause because of a severed driving wheel and its terrible mechanical condition in Barry scrapyard in the late 1970s, in 1980 the loco was bought only for parts to service sister engine *Leander* on the Severn Valley Railway. In 1990 all the disassembled parts were purchased by West Coast Railway Co in Carnforth and a long-term restoration, including casting new driving wheels, is well under way.

The main contribution of Barry LMS locos to the historical record has been the preservation of the two Somerset & Dorset 7F locomotives and the 2-6-0 Stanier 'Mogul'. None of the great LMS classes such as the 'Coronation', 'Princess Elizabeth' and 'Royal Scot' ended up at Barry, but thanks to Barry Butlin and private purchases direct from BR, examples of these magnificent engines still exist. Because the last bastion of working steam in 1968 was the North West of England, many LMS locos were purchased direct from BR at the end of steam; 12 LMS 'Black Five' locos were thus acquired. A number of LMS 8F War Department locos have also been repatriated from Turkey. More than 80 20th-century LMS locos still exist, so the contribution of the 35 Barry LMS locos is not quite as significant as that of the GWR or BR Standard locos, for example.

FACING PAGE TOP LMS Ivatt '2MT' 2-6-2T No 41312 departed from Barry in 1974 for the Caerphilly Railway Society. The locomotive was sold to a private buyer in the 1990s and is now a resident on the Mid Hants Railway. No 41312 is seen here with No 9466 and diesel No 20227 at Croxley on London Underground's Metropolitan Line, travelling from Amersham to Watford during May 2000 as part of LU's 'Steam on the Met' events. *Peter Brabham*

FACING PAGE BOTTOM No 42765 is the only restored example of the two LMS Hughes/Fowler 'Crab' locomotives that were sold for scrap at Barry. The locomotive left Barry in 1978 for use on the Keighley & Worth Valley Railway, but subsequently moved to the East Lancashire Railway. Here the locomotive is seen at Highley station during an autumn gala event on the Severn Valley Railway in September 2001. John Wiltshire

TOP LMS Stanier Mogul 2-6-0 No 42968 was the only extant example of its class in Barry scrapyard, and the only one now preserved. The locomotive was purchased for £3,575 in August 1973 by the Stanier Mogul Society and towed by rail to the Severn Valley Railway that December. It took 18 years to return to steam in April 1991 at a cost of £200,000, and since then the Mogul has been a regular service engine on the SVR, as well as making many main-line excursions, including jointly hauling the first preserved train to tackle the Lickey Incline in November 1997. Here the locomotive is seen at Dunster during a West Somerset Railway autumn gala in September 2007. *Peter Brabham*

ABOVE No 43924 has the distinction of being the very first locomotive to be purchased from Barry scrapyard, in September 1968. The locomotive is based on the Keighley & Worth Valley Railway, where its seen on shed at Haworth in 1993. After a major overhaul the locomotive returned to steam in 2011. *Peter Brabham*

RIGHT **LMS No 4422 (BR 44422) left Barry scrapyard in 1977 for the North Staffordshire Railway at Cheddleton, returning to steam in 1989. Since becoming operational again the locomotive has travelled around many preserved lines, and is seen here at Llangollen in 1994.** *Peter Brabham*

BELOW **Former LMS 'Black Five' No 45337 left Barry scrapyard in May 1984, the third of the six Class 5 locomotives to leave Barry. It was returned to steam on the East Lancashire Railway, but is also a regular locomotive on the North Yorkshire Moors. Here No 45337 is seen hauling a 'Santa Special' at Little Burrs on the East Lancashire line on Christmas Eve 2010. LMS 'Black Five' locomotives lasted right to the end of steam in the North West of England in 1968. For this reason, in addition to the six at Barry, 11 other 'Black Fives' were purchased direct from British Railways, and the prototype LMS No 5000 survives as part of the National Collection at York.** *Richard Fox*

ABOVE LMS 'Black Five' No 45379 left Barry in 1974 and was the first of the six examples of the class to leave the scrapyard. It was moved to Bitton, Bristol, for a slow restoration that commenced in 1979, returning to steam in 2010 after being moved to the Mid Hants Railway. Here the locomotive is seen on its first day of passenger operation at Alresford on 17 September 2010. *Peter Brabham*

FACING PAGE TOP LMS 'Jubilee' class No 5960 *Leander* (BR 45690) is one of the most famous locomotives rescued from Barry scrapyard. Purchased as a virtually intact engine in 1972 by Oliver, Taylor & Crossley, a private engineering company, for publicity purposes, the locomotive was commercially restored at BR's Derby Works in less than a year. Since that time it has changed hands many times and is now privately owned once more. A main-line certified engine for much of its preserved lifetime, it has worked all over the UK, and is seen here in September 2010 at a Severn Valley Railway autumn gala; the locomotive was resident on this line for most of the 1980s. *Peter Brabham*

FACING PAGE BOTTOM LMS Ivatt '2MT' No 46512 left Barry in 1973 for the Strathspey Railway in Scotland. Following a contract restoration by the Severn Valley Railway, the locomotive has been a regular on the Scottish tourist line, and returned to steam in 2011 after a major overhaul. Here it is seen on one of its first runs after overhaul in the spring of 2011. *Chris Boyd/Strathspey Railway*

FACING PAGE TOP Classmate No 46521 is seen here on shed at Toddington on the Gloucestershire Warwickshire Railway in August 1993. After spending only four years in the scrapyard, the locomotive left Barry in 1971 for the Severn Valley Railway in very good mechanical condition, returning to steam there in 1974. It is now based on the Great Central Railway, but is presently out of service. *Peter Brabham*

FACING PAGE BOTTOM 'Jinty' No 47327 was the sixth locomotive and the first of the class to leave Barry, in 1970. Purchased by Derby Corporation, it was subsequently based at the Midland Railway Centre at Butterley, where it is seen in April 1992. *Peter Brabham*

ABOVE LMS 0-6-0T 'Jinty' No 47279 was one of seven of these small shunting locomotives that were sent for scrap at Barry. The locomotive was purchased by the 3F Trust in 1979 for use on the Keighley & Worth Valley Railway, where it has been a regular service locomotive. It is seen on shed at Haworth in September 1988. *Peter Brabham*

TOP LMS 3F 'Jinty' 0-6-0 tank No 47493 found its way to Barry in June 1967 after spending its working life in the Liverpool area. It left Barry scrapyard in December 1972 for store in Radstock, Somerset, but a year later was moved by rail to the East Somerset Railway at Cranmore and, having returned to steam, pulled the inaugural train on that line in April 1980. For many years the locomotive was a regular service engine on the railway, as seen here at Cranmore shed. Since 2000 the engine has been located at the Spa Valley Railway near Tunbridge Wells. *Peter Brabham*

ABOVE LMS No 8431 (BR 48431) was one of six '8F' 2-8-0 locomotives sent for scrap at Barry, and was the first of the class to be purchased for preservation, in 1972, for the Keighley & Worth Valley Railway, where it is seen on Haworth shed in August 1983. *Peter Brabham*

TOP Former LMS No 48151 left Barry in 1975 after being privately purchased, and was based on the Yorkshire Dales Railway. Returning to steam in 1988, the locomotive is main-line certified and presently based at Carnforth for main-line running. Here it is seen on a main-line special at Seer Green & Jordans in April 2006. *David Brabham*

ABOVE LMS 2-8-0 No 8642 (BR 48642) left Barry in 1981 for the Peak Railway at Buxton, and took 28 years to restore to working order in 2009. The freight locomotive has caused quite a stir by being restored in LMS crimson red passenger livery, not the authentic plain black freight livery. Here it is seen at Irlam Vale station on the East Lancashire Railway in March 2010. *Allan Stoddern*

FACING PAGE TOP It was very fortunate that Barry scrapyard was the destination for two Somerset & Dorset Fowler '7F' 2-8-0 locomotives, as otherwise there would be no locomotives from this famous company in preservation. British Railways No 53808 was purchased from Barry for £2,500 in 1970 for restoration by the Somerset & Dorset Trust. After initially moving to Radstock, the locomotive relocated to Washford station on the West Somerset Railway in 1976, being returned to steam in August 1987. A regular performer on the WSR, No 88 is seen here looking splendid in its technically non-authentic S&DJR Prussian blue livery at the Gloucestershire Warwickshire Railway in June 2007. *Peter Brabham*

FACING PAGE BOTTOM Sister engine No 53809 was purchased from Barry in 1975 for restoration at the Midland Railway Centre at Butterley. Restored to steam in 1980, the locomotive had main-line certification for many years. It is now a service locomotive on the North Yorkshire Moors Railway, as seen here in mundane BR black livery at Grosmont station in July 2010. *Peter Brabham*

TOP The Somerset & Dorset line, over which many Barry locomotives worked until the closure of the line in the mid-1960s, owes a great debt of gratitude to Barry scrapyard, resulting in many heritage lines being able to re-create classic S&D combinations. Here No 53808 and BR Standard No 73906 re-create a classic S&D scene at Medstead & Four Marks station on the Mid Hants Railway in September 2010. *Peter Brabham*

ABOVE On 24 March 2006 sister engines Nos 53808 and 53809 power out of Bishops Lydeard station on the West Somerset Railway in thunderous weather conditions. *Peter Brabham*

8 | London & North Eastern Railway steam locomotive purchased from Barry scrapyard

LNER locomotive classes are not that well represented in preservation, except for the six examples of the famous 'A4' class. Apart from the few 20th century LNER locomotives in the National Collection, including No 4468 *Mallard*, it was down to the foresight of a few individuals and societies in the early 1960s that purchased LNER locomotives such as No 60532 *Blue Peter* direct from British Railways, that we still have working LNER locomotives to enjoy today. The only example of a locomotive built by the LNER that ended up at Barry scrapyard was Thompson 'B1' class 4-6-0 No 61264. The engine did not arrive at the yard direct from withdrawal from BR service in 1965. It arrived later in 1968, because after withdrawal it was abused as a stationary boiler for a few years, resulting in the locomotive's boiler ending up in very poor condition. The engine was purchased from Barry in 1976 by the B1 Trust and moved to the Great Central Railway. The boiler was lagged in blue asbestos which had limited its close inspection at Barry. On professional removal of the asbestos, it was discovered that the boiler was in a very bad way, being thick with rust and with a badly wasted firebox. This setback could have immediately stopped the locomotive's restoration; in fact it took six years to find a firm capable of tackling the boiler repairs. The total restoration cost back to steam was estimated to be around £230,000. The LNER 'B1' locomotive finally returned to steam in March 1997 at Loughborough. In 1999, with mainline certification, the locomotive hauled summer tourist trains from Fort William to Mallaig and saw service on heritage lines until the locomotive's boiler certification expired in 2008. Another major overhaul was completed in 2012 and over £400,000 has been spent on a new inner firebox and boiler parts manufactured in Germany to return the locomotive back to steam.

British Railways Standard steam locomotives purchased from Barry scrapyard

In total, 38 locomotives built by British Railways after nationalisation were purchased from Barry scrapyard, and their types and numbers are listed below. The numbers in **bold** indicate locomotives that have been returned to steam, but may currently be in store out of boiler certification or under overhaul.

2-6-4 tank locomotives
80064 80072 80078 80079 80080 80097 **80098** 80100 **80104 80105 80135 80136** 80150 **80151**

2-6-0 Class 2 tender locomotives
78018 **78019 78022** 78059

2-6-0 Class 4 tender locomotives
76017 76077 **76079 76084**

4-6-0 Class 4MT tender locomotives
75014 75069 75078 75079

4-6-0 Class 5MT tender locomotives
73082 73096 73129 73156

4-6-2 Class 8P tender locomotive
71000

2-10-0 Class 9F tender locomotives
92134 92207 **92212 92214** 92219 **92240** 92245

The jewel in the crown in the list is, of course, the unique No 71000 *Duke of Gloucester*, the last 'Pacific' loco to be constructed in Britain.

The 14 Standard 2-6-4 tank locomotives have proved to be one of the most popular classes of locomotive purchased from Barry scrapyard for use on heritage lines. This is due to their versatility and good power-to-running-cost ratio, which is exactly why they were designed by British Railways.

Without the contribution of the 38 Barry locos, British Railways Standard engines would be poorly represented in Britain's heritage pool. In fact, there would only be eight in existence, including *Britannia*, *Oliver Cromwell*, David Shepherd's 9F *Black Prince*, and BR's last-constructed steam loco, *Evening Star* – a very poor historical sample.

Fourteen British Railways Standard 4MT 2-6-4 tank engines were sent for scrap to Barry. The oldest of them, No 80064, left Barry in 1973 for the South Devon Railway, being restored by 1981. After running on the Paignton & Dartmouth Railway for a few years, as seen here in 1983, the locomotive was moved to the Bluebell Railway, where it has been a regular service engine but is presently out of service. *Peter Brabham*

TOP After purchase by the Southern Steam Trust, BR Standard No 80078 left Barry in 1976 for the Swanage Railway. Restored to steam by 1999, the engine has been a regular service engine on the line, as seen above, entering Corfe in the summer of 2006. *Peter Brabham*

ABOVE No 80072 is the latest of many of the big BR Standard tanks to return to steam. It left Barry in 1988, the 206th locomotive to depart, and was in terrible condition, even missing a wheelset. It proved to be a major and very expensive restoration project by the Llangollen Standard Four Project, culminating in the magnificent restoration of the engine on the Llangollen line by 2009. Here the locomotive poses in the afternoon sun at Carrog in September 2010. *Peter Brabham*

TOP BR Standard No 80080, hauling a BR Network SouthEast-liveried Class 308 unit, approaches Rickmansworth while running north from Harrow-on-the-Hill to Amersham during London Underground's Metropolitan Line 'Steam on the Met' event in May 1990. The Class 308 unit is more usually found working between Liverpool Street and Shenfield. No 80080 left Barry in 1980 and restored by the Princess Royal Class Locomotive Trust at Butterley. Running with main-line certification, it has seen work all over the BR network, including back at Barry and up the South Wales valleys. *David Brabham*

ABOVE In 1971, BR Standard No 80079 became the first of the class to leave Barry, for the Severn Valley Railway, after being assessed as the example in the best mechanical condition. Returned to steam by 1977, the locomotive has been a regular SVR service engine, even making main-line excursions. Here No 80079 is seen at a gala event in 1998 at Bewdley station on the SVR. The engine's boiler certification subsequently expired and it was put on static display. In 2011, No 80079 was purchased for £250,000 by multi-millionaire investment banker Jeremy Hosking, who has now to foot the bill for the expensive overhaul back to working order on the SVR. *Peter Brabham*

TOP BR Standard No 80136 left Barry in 1979 for the North Staffordshire Railway at Cheddleton. The locomotive is seen here on loan to the West Somerset Railway, carrying out demonstration shunting at Dunster goods depot in April 2007. *Peter Brabham*

ABOVE BR standard 2-6-4 tank locomotive 80105 left Woodham scrapyard as long ago as 1973 being the third locomotive of this class to leave, of the 14 that were present in the scrapyard. No 80105 was built at Brighton Works in 1955 and had spent its working life in east London, finally ending up on the Cambrian coast line of Wales from 1962 until withdrawal in 1965. The

locomotive was purchased by a group of members of the Scottish Railway Preservation Society for use on their Bo'ness & Kinneil Railway, a heritage railway line that has been developed on a green-field site by the south shore of the Firth of Forth in Scotland. The locomotive's restoration started in 1992 and the locomotive was returned to steam by December 1999. The 10-year boiler certification for the large BR tank locomotive subsequently expired in 2010 and the locomotive is now out of service pending a second major overhaul. 80105 is seen above out on loan to the Strathspey Steam Railway and is captured arriving at Boat of Garten station on a train from Aviemore in June 1988. *Gordon Thompson*

ABOVE BR Standard No 80135 was built at Brighton Works in 1956 and withdrawn in 1965. It left Barry in 1973 for the North Yorkshire Moors Railway, returning to steam in BR green livery in April 1980; it is seen at Levisham station in April 1984. After many miles of service on the NYMR in the 1980s, the locomotive is presently out of service. No 80135 was restored with a steel firebox, which proved troublesome and is to be replaced with a copper example. *Peter Brabham*

FACING PAGE TOP LEFT BR Standard tank No 80104 left Barry in 1984 for use on the Swanage Railway. After being untouched for five years, the locomotive was moved to Swindon Works, where restoration was begun by Southern Locomotives Ltd. After being evicted from Swindon, it was moved to the Avon Valley Railway in 1991. Moving back to the Swanage Railway in 1995, it was finally restored for use on that line in April 1997. No 80104 is seen here at Swanage station during a night gala event on 12 September 2008; the photo is a little homage to the greatest railway photographer of them all, O. Winston Link. *Peter Brabham*

FACING PAGE TOP RIGHT BR '2MT' 2-6-0 No 78022 was purchased by the Standard Locomotive Preservation Society in 1975. It returned to steam on the Keighley & Worth Valley Railway in 1992, and is seen there on shed at Haworth. *Peter Brabham*

FACING PAGE BOTTOM BR Standard tank No 80151 enters Sheffield Park station on the Bluebell Railway in August 2011. The locomotive left Barry in 1975 for the Stour Valley Railway in Essex, later moving to the Bluebell Railway, where it returned to steam in 2001. *Peter Brabham*

ABOVE British Railways Standard '2MT' 2-6-0 No 78019 was originally purchased in 1973 for the Severn Valley Railway, but worked subsequently on the Great Central Railway from 2004. Here the locomotive is seen back on the SVR at a gala event in March 2010. *Peter Brabham*

FACING PAGE TOP BR Standard '4MT' 2-6-0 No 76079 is one of the most travelled ex-Barry steam locomotives in the UK. Privately purchased from Barry in 1974 for the failed Steamport Southport heritage project, the locomotive was sold on to Ian Riley and ran with main-line certification for many years, as seen here in August 2009, travelling over Barmouth Viaduct. The locomotive was subsequently sold on to the North Yorkshire Moors Railway and used as a service engine capable of working to Whitby over Network Rail tracks. *Peter Brabham*

FACING PAGE BOTTOM Another view of No 76079 working over the picturesque Barmouth Viaduct on the Cambrian Coast line in August 2009. *Peter Brabham*

LEFT BR Standard 4MT No 76017 was built in 1953 and had only 12 years of BR service before being withdrawn. It was purchased by the Standard Four Group and left Barry in 1975, originally for Buckinghamshire, but it later moved on to the Mid Hants Railway, where it ran from 1984 to 1997; it is seen here working hard up Ropley bank in the winter snow of December 1990. The locomotive has been out of service for 14 years, but has recently entered the works for a major overhaul. *Peter Brabham*

THIS PAGE TOP BR Standard '4MT' 4-6-0 No 75014 was purchased from Barry in 1981 for use on the North Yorkshire Moors Railway, and was returned to steam in 1995 with main-line certification. The engine saw use on the summer Fort William to Mallaig tourist trains in 1995-98, and is seen here in 1995 at Amersham during a London Underground 'Steam on the Met' event. No 75014 was subsequently sold to the Paignton & Dartmouth Railway and named *Braveheart* for use in the few last years of its boiler certification. It is presently in the restoration queue on the Dartmouth line. *Peter Brabham*

THIS PAGE BOTTOM BR Standard '4MT' 4-6-0 No 75069 was built at Swindon in 1955 and withdrawn in 1967. It was an early restoration project, being transported by rail from Barry in 1973 for the Severn Valley Railway. A regular service locomotive on the SVR for many years with periods of main-line certification, No 75069 is seen here in the setting sun at Kidderminster station in 1989. *Peter Brabham*

TOP British Railways Standard No 75078 was the first of the four examples of this class at Barry to leave, in 1972. Restored to full operation by the Standard Four Society on the Keighley & Worth Valley Railway by 1977, the locomotive is seen here being prepared for service on shed at Haworth at Easter 1990. It was a regular performer on the K&WVR, but is presently out of certification and under overhaul again. *Peter Brabham*

ABOVE British Railways Standard '5MT' 4-6-0 No 73096 is here masquerading as long-scrapped sister engine No 73052 at a Somerset & Dorset event on the West Somerset Railway in 1995. No 73096 was privately purchased from Barry in 1985, moving to the Mid Hants Railway for full restoration by 1993; it is now a regular service engine on that line. *Peter Brabham*

TOP British Railways Standard '5MT' No 73129 is on the West Somerset Railway at Williton in March 2006, working in tandem with David Shepherd's '9F' No 92203 *Black Prince*, which was purchased direct from BR. No 73129 was the only Caprotti-valve-geared example of this '5MT' class in Barry scrapyard. After purchase in 1973 by Derby Corporation as a heritage project, the locomotive left Barry for Derby Works, and full restoration subsequently took place at the Midland Railway Centre, Butterley, with the engine returning to steam in 2005. *Peter Brabham*

ABOVE British Railways Standard '5MT' No 73082 *Camelot* was purchased from Barry in 1979 by the Camelot Society, based on the Bluebell Railway. This 1986 view shows the locomotive in steam at Sheffield Park station on the Bluebell Line, but it is presently out of boiler certification and undergoing another major overhaul. *Peter Brabham*

FACING PAGE TOP The magnificence of the restoration of *Duke of Gloucester* is shown at its best in the early morning sunshine passing the Highley Engine House museum during a Severn Valley Railway gala in March 2009. *Peter Brabham*

FACING PAGE BOTTOM The unique British Standard Pacific No 71000 *Duke of Gloucester* was purchased by the 71000 Duke of Gloucester Locomotive Trust in 1974. Devoid of many parts, including its unique cylinders and its tender, the restoration was called 'mission impossible' by sceptics. However, after a long and expensive restoration at Loughborough, 'the Duke' triumphantly returned to steam on 11 November 1986. Here No 71000 is captured attacking Hatton bank in early morning sunshine in 1992. *David Brabham*

ABOVE Nine of the mighty British Railways Standard '9F' 2-10-0 freight locomotives were sent to Barry for scrap, and two were cut up on the site. Of the seven remaining, three have been restored to steam, all of which have been very expensive restoration projects. No 92212 left Barry in 1979, at a purchase price of £10,000, for the Great Central Railway, returning to steam by 1995. The locomotive was then sold to a private purchaser and moved to the Mid Hants Railway, where it is in regular service. No 92212 is seen here on 19 September 2010 at Medstead & Four Marks station on the Mid Hants line. *Peter Brabham*

FACING PAGE TOP No 92214 left Barry in 1980 for the Peak Railway Centre. It was restored by 2004 and moved to the Midland Railway Centre at Butterley for operation. After moving to the North Yorkshire Moors Railway for operation in 2010, the engine was jointly purchased by a driver and fireman working on the NYMR. Here the mighty '9F' is seen being prepared for operation at Grosmont shed in July 2010. *Peter Brabham*

FACING PAGE BOTTOM British Standard '9F' No 92240 was the first of this type of locomotive to leave Barry scrapyard, in 1978, after a £10,500 purchase by the 9F Preservation Group, based on the Bluebell Railway. The locomotive had no tender in Barry scrapyard and a new one had to be built on a salvaged frame. Missing parts were acquired from David Shepherd, the owner of No 92203 *Black Prince*, who had purchased spare parts from BR at the end of steam. No 92240 was returned to steam by September 1990 and is seen here waiting for the off at Sheffield Park station on the Bluebell Railway in May 1992. In 2012 the locomotive returned to the Bluebell line with another ten-year boiler certificate. *Peter Brabham*

ABOVE The mighty BR Standard '9F' 2-10-0 locomotives were designed as the ultimate heavy freight locomotives, hauling freight trains all over the UK, such as the legendary Tyne Dock to Consett iron-ore traffic in the North East of England. However, some '9Fs' found passenger work on the Somerset & Dorset line, and briefly on Cardiff to London summer trains in the 1960s. Although the two '9F' locomotives preserved directly from BR, Nos 92220 *Evening Star* and 92203 *Black Prince*, were allowed on the main line in the 1970s and '80s, '9Fs' are now banned from main-line work due to their flangeless centre driving wheel, so their full potential is rarely realised on heritage lines. In June 1998 two '9Fs', Barry scrapyard restoration No 92212 and David Shepherd's No 92203 *Black Prince*, were put through their paces hauling a demonstration stone train at Merehead Quarry. Truly this was a fantastic spectacle in terms of both sight and sound. *Peter Brabham*

The 'Barry 10' and the unrestored locomotives

The 213 locomotives that were not cut up at Barry represented examples of the 'Big Four' pre-nationalisation companies, the Great Western, Southern, London Midland & Scottish and London & North Eastern, as well as the nationalised British Railways. The ratio is shown in the accompanying chart.

By 2011, 64% of the Barry locos had returned to steam. Interestingly, apart from the single LNER locomotive, the preservation ratios of the other locomotives are virtually identical: GWR 62%, Southern 63%, LMS 66%, and BR 65%.

Of the 77 Barry locomotives that are still unrestored, some are coming to the end of a long-term restoration and should be working again in the next few years:

- GWR 2-6-2T No 4150 at the Severn Valley Railway
- GWR 2-8-0T No 4270 at the Gloucestershire Warwickshire Railway
- GWR No 7202 at the Great Western Society, Didcot
- GWR No 6989 *Wightwick Hall* at the Buckinghamshire Railway Centre, Quainton Road
- Southern Railway No 34058 *Sir Fredrick Pile* at Swanage
- Southern Railway No 35006 *Peninsular and Oriental S. N. Co* at the Gloucester & Warwickshire Railway.
- LMS 'Black Five' 4-6-0 No 45491 at the Great Central Railway
- LMS No 45699 *Galatea* by the West Coast Railway Co at Carnforth
- BR 5MT 4-6-0 No 73156 at Bury
- BR 4MT 2-6-0 No 76084 restored at Morpeth but completed at the North Norfolk Railway
- BR 9F 2-10-0 No 92134 at LNWR, Crewe

There are also examples of locomotives purchased with great expectations of restoration that sadly still remain untouched. Of these, the most notorious are the 'Barry 10', purchased with an £85,000 grant from the National Heritage Memorial Fund in 1988 for a planned Wales Railway Centre that never happened. The locos were moved to Butetown, Cardiff Bay, in 1988, but when it was obvious that the Cardiff Bay Redevelopment Plan did not include a heritage railway, they were moved back to Barry in 1994, initially being stored in a warehouse and later moving again to Barry railway depot. In 2011/12 seven of the 'Barry 10' locos were dispersed to various restoration centres, mainly to be dismantled for spares. The 'Barry 10' locos were:

Loco	Wheel arrangement	Class	Built	Withdrawn
GWR No 2861	2-8-0	'28XX'	1918	1963
GWR No 4115	2-6-2T	'5101'	1936	1965
GWR No 5227	2-8-0T	'52XX'	1924	1963
GWR No 5539	2-6-2T	'45XX'	1928	1962
GWR No 6686	0-6-2T	'66XX'	1928	1964
GWR No 7929 Willington Hall	4-6-0	'Hall'	1918	1963
LMS No 48518	2-8-0	8F	1944	1965
LMS No 44901	4-6-0	'Black Five'	1945	1965
BR No 80150	2-6-4T	4MT	1956	1965
BR No 92245	2-10-0	9F	1958	1964

Of the unrestored Barry locomotives, probably the one that GWR enthusiasts would like to see running again is the last of the five GWR 'Castles', No 7029 *Thornbury Castle*. The loco left Barry as far back as 1972 for the Birmingham Railway Museum, and is now owned by Pete Waterman and in store at the Crewe Heritage Centre.

One locomotive that has come back from the dead is LMS 'Jubilee' class No 45699 *Galatea*, given up as a lost cause back in the 1980s, mainly because of its severed driving wheel and general terrible external condition. The loco was initially only bought from Barry in 1980 to use as spare parts for another 'Jubilee', No 45960 *Leander*, but the parts were sold on in the 1990s and active restoration of the loco to main-line standards is under way by West Coast Railway Co at Carnforth shed, potentially for completion by 2012/13.

Another interesting Barry locomotive story is that of LMS Ivatt No 41313, which was purchased from Barry in 1972 as a virtually intact locomotive. It was stored untouched in a shed at the Buckinghamshire Railway Centre for 34 years as a source of spares for a classmate purchased direct from BR at the end of steam. In 2006 No

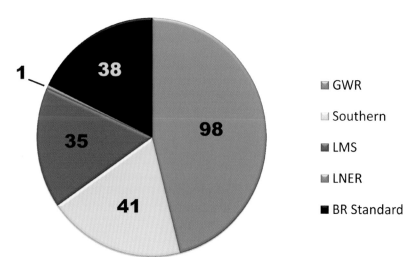

- ◼ GWR
- ◻ Southern
- ◼ LMS
- ◼ LNER
- ◼ BR Standard

41313 was moved by ferry to the Isle of Wight Railway for a long-term restoration programme to return it to steam to work on the island's heritage line.

In 1987, in the final period of Barry scrapyard, five locomotives of GWR origin were purchased by businessman Tony Rippingale and moved to the Pontypool & Blaenavon Railway. These became known as the 'Blaenavon Five' and were stored out in the open near the Big Pit national mining museum. They remained largely untouched for 20 years until 2007, when they were put up for sale, except for No 5668, which remains at Blaenavon for long-term restoration. The five locos were GWR 2-8-0 No 2874, now at the West Somerset Railway, GWR 2-8-0 No 3855, now at the East Lancashire Railway, GWR 2-8-0T No 4253, now at the Kent & East Sussex Railway, GWR 0-6-2T No 5668, still at Blaenavon under long-term restoration, and GWR 4-6-0 No 5967 *Bickmarsh Hall*, now at the Northampton & Lamport Railway.

LEFT The remains of 'Barry 10' BR 'Black Five' No 44901 stand outside Barry shed, also in May 2010. In 2012 this hulk became the subject of a restoration appeal which would be quite a formidable task. *Peter Brabham*

BELOW 'Barry 10' GWR 2-8-0 tank No 5227 is lost in the undergrowth behind Barry shed in April 2011. The locomotive was subsequently moved to the GWS at Didcot, where it became a parts donor for the Great Western Society's proposed building of a GWR 2-8-0 '47xx' mixed traffic 'Night Owl'. *Peter Brabham*

ABOVE The skeletal remains of 'Barry 10' BR Standard No 80150 stand alongside Barry shed in July 2010. The locomotive was subsequently swapped for a turntable for use at Barry depot, and No 80150 is now on the Mid Hants Railway for restoration. *Peter Brabham*

TOP This was the last view of 'Barry 10' GWR No 7927 *Willington Hall* in September 2005, before it was dismantled for the construction of new-build GWR 'Grange' and 'County' locomotives. *Peter Brabham*

TOP Unrestored GWR 2-8-0T No 4270 languishes in a siding at the Swansea Vale
Railway in 1996. The large Great Western tank locomotive had been purchased
and moved from Barry in 1985, and is now owned by multi-millionaire Jeremy
Hosking. It was moved to the Gloucestershire Warwickshire Railway in 2003,
where it is currently nearing the completion of a long-term restoration.
Peter Brabham

ABOVE BR 2-10-0 '9F' No 92219 was purchased and removed from Barry
scrapyard in 1985. Twenty-five years later, in July 2010, the locomotive still
stands totally untouched at the Midland Railway Centre, Butterley, and is
under threat of being dismantled for parts. *Peter Brabham*

TOP GWR 2-8-0 No 2874, built in November 1918, is seen with the rest of the 'Blaenavon Five' stored out in the open in the late 1990s on the Pontypool & Blaenavon Railway. The locomotive was purchased by the Dinmore Manor Group, which owns classmate No 3850, and moved to the West Somerset Railway in 2007, where it is now the subject of a long-term restoration appeal. *Peter Brabham*

ABOVE Lurking at the back of a shed in deepest rural Buckinghamshire in July 2012, the restoration of the 92 tons of GWR 2-8-2 tank engine No 7200 makes progress. Originally built in 1930 as GWR 2-8-0 tank No 5275, the locomotive was modified in 1934 into a 2-8-2 tank with a larger coal and water capacity and numbered 7200, the prototype of its class. After nearly 30 years of hauling South

Wales coal and Cornish China clay trains, No 7200 was withdrawn from traffic by British Railways in 1963. The locomotive was purchased from Woodham Brothers in 1981 and moved to the Buckinghamshire Railway Centre at Quainton Road. The restoration of the large tank engine only began in earnest in 1996 with the formation of the 7200 Trust. So far £200,000 has been spent on the restoration of the chassis and cylinders. As can be seen the bottom half of the locomotive and tanks are now near completion. However the restoration task ahead is still daunting, as the boiler requires a further £50,000 of professional attention, it being now nearly 50 years since it was last steamed. It is a formidable task raising the necessary funds to fully restore this impressive machine back to steam. *Peter Brabham*

ABOVE The dedication to the cause of preserving ex-Barry scrapyard locomotives is shown here by GWR 'Large Prairie' No 4150, in the process of restoration under a canvas tent at Bewdley station on the Severn Valley Railway. The locomotive left Barry as long ago as 1974, arriving at the Severn Valley in 1978 via the Dean Forest Railway. Since this photograph was taken in the autumn of 2010 the tanks have been fabricated and the locomotive is well on its way to working once again. *Peter Brabham*

GWR No 6989 *Wightwick Hall* was allocated in the Worcester and Hereford area for most of its working life and often pulled the 'Cambrian Coast Express' and 'Cathedrals Express' named trains until withdrawal, when it was towed to Barry scrapyard from Gloucester in August 1964. The locomotive was purchased by the Wightwick Hall Restoration Group and moved in January 1978 to the Buckinghamshire Railway Centre at Quainton Road. A long restoration is now reaching its climax and a hydraulic boiler test was expected at the end of 2012. *Wightwick Hall* should be seen working again in the foreseeable future. *Peter Brabham*

ABOVE GWR 'Small Prairie' tank No 5532 is under restoration in the busy Llangollen Railway shed in 2010. After leaving Barry in 1981, sister locomotives Nos 5532 and 5538 were evaluated at the Dean Forest Railway and the best parts of each were selected to restore No 5532. Only now, 30 years later, has the restoration begun. *Peter Brabham*

LEFT The ongoing long-term restoration of LMS Fowler '4F' 0-6-0 No 44123 is glimpsed under a plastic tent at the Avon Valley Railway in autumn 2012. The locomotive, a regular on the Somerset & Dorset Railway in the 1950s, was withdrawn in 1965 and purchased for scrap by Woodham Brothers. After 16 years in the scrapyard, No 44123 was moved from Barry in December 1981, initially to the Mid Hants Railway, moving again five years later in May 1986 to the Bitton site. To date, the locomotive's tender has been restored and much of the restoration of other locomotive parts and fittings has been completed. *Peter Brabham*

FACING PAGE TOP **The only class of locomotive from Barry scrapyard where no representative has so far been returned to steam is the big GWR 2-8-2T heavy freight tanks of the '72XX' class. Of the three Barry scrapyard examples, Nos 7200, 7202 and 7229, No 7202 looks the most likely to return to steam in the short term. The Great Western Society at Didcot was tempted to buy No 7200, the prototype of the class, but No 7202 was mechanically the best of the three. It was originally built in 1930 as 2-8-0 No 5277, but the changing South Wales coal market required a locomotive with a larger coal capacity. After being put in store until 1934, it was rebuilt with extended frames and bunker and a trailing wheel. No 7202 left Barry in April 1974 and is seen here in scrapyard condition at the Didcot site in 1977.** *Hedley Davies*

FACING PAGE BOTTOM **The ongoing restoration of No 7202 at Didcot, seen here in 2010, has taken more than 30 years, and the sight of a working mighty '72XX' tank again is eagerly anticipated by all GWR enthusiasts.** *Peter Brabham*

THISPAGE TOP **Competing for finances for new Barry scrapyard restorations are locomotives previously restored but now out of boiler certification and requiring another major overhaul. A typical example is No 7820 *Dinmore Manor*, looking a bit sad in March 2008 on display at Minehead on the West Somerset Railway.** *Peter Brabham*

THIS PAGE BOTTOM **Providing a good impersonation of Newport Docks *circa* 1965 are these three ex-Barry scrapyard Bulleid Pacifics, now all out of boiler certification. Nos 35005 *Canadian Pacific*, 34016 *Bodmin* and 34105 *Swanage* stand in the cramped yard at Ropley shed on the Mid Hants Railway in September 2010.** *Peter Brabham*

11

The next phase – the rebuild projects

By 2011 a representative of every steam locomotive class saved from Barry scrapyard except one had returned to steam. None of the three large GWR '72XX' 2-8-2 tank locomotives purchased have yet steamed, although this could be rectified in the next two years with the finalisation of the long-term restoration of No 7202 at Didcot. Therefore all Barry locomotive restoration projects in future will create duplicates of existing loco types.

If long-lost locomotive classes are to be created, there are two options. First, unlimited financial resources can be sourced to build any steam locomotive from scratch. The creation of new-build LNER 'A1' 'Pacific' *Tornado* has shown that it is now technically feasible, given the funding, to create a brand-new locomotive from scratch using official plans and drawings. Second, new locomotive types can be created at a much lower cost using the interchangeable parts of unrestored Barry locomotives.

Given the general very poor mechanical state of the surviving but as yet unrestored locomotives scattered around the UK, preservationists are looking at such possibilities. The Great Western Railway had a philosophy of standardisation for its fleet of locomotives, which means that many parts are interchangeable between classes.

This chapter will look at what progress has been made so far with ongoing rebuild projects around the UK and how the legacy of ex-Barry locomotives has been key to many of these projects.

The West Somerset Railway decided to build a versatile small tender locomotive from a Barry scrapyard locomotive, using GWR '5101' class 'Large Prairie' tank No 5193 to create a brand new GWR 2-6-0 tender class. The new locomotive has a 6-ton coal capacity rather than the 4 tons of the original. With much increased footplate space compared with the original 'Prairie', it can be used more easily for driver training. Such a GWR Mogul tender locomotive was conceived but never actually built by the GWR. No 5193 left Barry scrapyard in 1979 for Steamport Southport, but the remains were then re-sold to the West Somerset Railway for this project. The brand new No 5193 entered service in September 2004 and is seen here at Bewdley station visiting the Severn Valley Railway for an autumn gala in September 2005.
Peter Brabham

TOP Great Western Railway 'Saint' class 2-6-0 No 2920 *Saint David*, built in August 1907 and withdrawn from service in 1953, is seen here at Swindon on an unknown date but carrying a British Railways livery. The GWR 'Saint' class was designed by George Jackson Churchward and built from 1902 as 4-6-0 passenger locomotives; 76 were built, and the successful 4-6-0 design paved the way for the later 'Star', 'Hall', 'Castle' and 'King' class locomotives. The 'Saints' were withdrawn between 1931 and 1953, and scrapped at Swindon Works. Although one member of the 1907 GWR 'Star' class, *Lode Star*, is part of the National Collection at York, no GWR 'Saint' class locomotive made it into preservation. The 'Saint' rebuild project is well under way at the Great Western Society at Didcot, and involves the 'back conversion' of the remains of Barry scrapyard locomotive No 4942 *Maindy Hall* into new 'Saint' class locomotive No 2999, to be named *Lady of Legend*. *Colour-Rail*

ABOVE GWR Hawksworth 'County' class No 1011 *County of Chester* stands at Cardiff East Dock in July 1964. Cardiff Canton steam depot (88A) closed to steam on 9 September 1962, and all steam engines were then transferred down the docks to East Dock shed (88L) until its closure in 1965. *County of Chester* was the last working example of this class of 30 locomotives; built in January 1946, it was cut up at Cashmore's, Newport, in March 1965. Of the 30 'Counties', 16 were cut up in South Wales, but unfortunately by chance none ended up in Barry scrapyard. The Great Western Society at Didcot noted that there were sufficient standard GWR 'parts' existing from unrestored Barry scrapyard locomotives to re-create the basis of a 'County' locomotive. The rebuild project will utilise the frames of 'Modified Hall' No 7927 *Willington Hall* and the boiler of LMS No 48518, both locomotives being part of the infamous 'Barry 10' in long-term storage in South Wales. Both locomotives were under the ownership of Vale of Glamorgan Council, so it has been agreed that the completed locomotive will recreate No 1014 *County of Glamorgan*, which was cut up at Cashmore's scrapyard in Newport in December 1964. *John Wiltshire*

ABOVE GWR No 6810 *Blakemere Grange*, seen at Bedminster, Bristol, on 19 October 1962, was one of the 80 'Grange' class locomotives built between 1936 and 1939. It was cut up at Bird's scrapyard in Bridgend, South Wales, in February 1965. All the 'Granges' were cut up between 1960 and 1965, 27 of them in South Wales, but none were sent to Barry scrapyard. The 6880 Betton Grange Society, based at the Llangollen Railway, was formed in 1998 with the intention of re-creating a Great Western 'Grange' class locomotive. For this purpose it has cut brand new frames, and purchased the remains of No 5952 *Cogan Hall* and the boiler of No 7927 *Willington Hall*. It has also obtained three 5ft 8in wheelsets from GWR 'Prairie' No 4156; this locomotive was cut up at Barry in 1980, but the wheelsets were purchased by the Severn Valley Railway for use as 'spares'. Project fundraising involves a bi-annual steam spectacular gala event on the Llangollen Railway. *John Wiltshire*

FACING PAGE TOP Although Barry scrapyard had a good representative sample of British Railways Standard locomotives, including 14 of the large '4MT' 2-6-2 tanks of the '80XXX' class, there were no examples of the smaller '82XXX' and '84XXX' class 2-6-2 tanks. This was pure chance, as examples of both classes were cut up at nearby Newport. Here we see a suitable grimy example, No 82040, at Bedminster, Bristol, on 19 October 1963. No 82040 was cut up at Bird's, Long Marston, in September 1965. Two projects are proposed to create both these lost types, with the 82045 project at the Severn Valley Railway and an 84000 project on the Bluebell Railway. BR Standard Class 2MT 2-6-0 tender locomotive No 78059 was purchased by the Bluebell Railway from Woodham's scrapyard in 1980; it had no tender, as that had been sold to the Duport Steelworks at Briton Ferry to carry ingots. In 1994 the Bluebell Railway announced that this locomotive would form the basis of a conversion to an '84XXX' tank engine. The 82045 project on the Severn Valley is essentially a new-build project, which may incorporate parts of ex-Barry locomotives. This is appropriate as ten members of the '82XXX' class were allocated to Barry depot in 1955. *John Wiltshire*

FACING PAGE BOTTOM LMS unrebuilt 'Patriot' 5XP 4-6-0 No 45519 *Lady Godiva*, built in February 1933, passes through Longsight station, Manchester, in June 1957. This locomotive was withdrawn from Bristol Barrow Road in March 1962. None of the unrebuilt 'Patriots' were sold to scrapyards, all being cut up by British Railways at Crewe Works. The LMS Patriot project based at the Llangollen Railway aims to re-create a unrebuilt 'Patriot' locomotive. It began in November 2010 with the restoration of a Fowler tender acquired from Vale of Glamorgan Council and stored at the Barry Railway Centre, South Wales. At today's prices this project could cost £1.5 million. Essentially it will be a new locomotive with a small part of Barry scrapyard in it, pulling a tender from Woodham Brothers. *Colour-Rail*

12 Steam returns to South Wales

There is absolutely no doubt that the remarkable availability of the 213 Barry scrapyard locomotives sparked off numerous railway heritage lines around the UK. The early examples from the 1960s, such as the Bluebell, Keighley & Worth Valley, Didcot, Severn Valley, South Devon and North Yorkshire Moors lines, were a haven for locomotives purchased directly from British Railways at the end of steam. In the 1970s new lines were opened that now rely virtually entirely on ex-Barry locomotives for hauling their tourist trains; examples include heritage lines such as the Mid Hants, Dartmouth, Gloucester & Warwickshire, Swanage, Great Central and Llangollen. Not all heritage lines are 'chocolate box' recreations in rural England; heritage lines such as the East Lancashire and the Great Central have proven successful in a more industrial context.

South Wales was home to the first steam railway train in the world (1804) and the world's first passenger railway at Mumbles, Swansea (1809). Wales also has the magnificent narrow gauge slate lines such as the Ffestiniog, Talyllyn and Welsh Highland in North Wales, as well as the Snowdon Mountain Railway. However, Wales is the only UK country not to have a transport museum. No working GWR locomotive can be found within the South Wales coalfield or in Wales' capital city, not even a cosmetically restored TVR, GWR or BR locomotive for the younger generation to study as part of their education.

In 1987 there was great enthusiasm for a Wales Railway Centre to be built in Cardiff Bay, which would supplement the Welsh Industrial & Maritime Museum that was built in 1977 to trigger regeneration of the derelict docks. However, in the late 1980s heritage was not to be part of the great master plan for the regeneration of Cardiff Bay, even though the very existence of modern Cardiff is solely due to the coal export trade. The Welsh Industrial & Maritime Museum was sold off to developers and the 'Barry 10' locos, which were to form the basis of the planned railway centre, were put back in store at Barry in 1988. Sadly, in much the same way the Swansea Vale Railway in the centre of Swansea was closed in 2007 when the City Council decided to redevelop the land.

The Vale of Glamorgan Railway at Barry was formed in 1995 and made good progress in developing a heritage line as part of the Barry Docks and Island regeneration. The sight of visiting ex-Barry GWR locos working back at Barry was truly a fantastic sight. However, in 2007 the Vale of Glamorgan Council withdrew its financial support for the project, evicting the volunteers and handing the lease to Cambrian Transport. Although Barry has huge potential as a heritage rail centre, with a few miles of running track, and as a rail depot for main-line specials, it will take a lot of effort to regenerate the project. The majority of the 'Barry 10' locos have now been dispersed to other projects around the UK, and only two locos are staying at Barry with the aim of restoration.

In 2000 Blaenavon was granted UNESCO World Heritage status for its industrial landscape and the superb Big Pit mining museum. The Pontypool & Blaenavon heritage railway, which since 1980 has run industrial locos over three-quarters of a mile of track, has now suddenly received grant aid attention; the line has been extended, bridges repaired, a short spur line to Big Pit constructed, and the future looks rosy with visiting GWR tank locomotives pounding up the South Wales valley in their true context.

This final chapter is my personal photographic tribute to the ex-Barry locomotives that have returned to South Wales to give pleasure to the local enthusiasts that were first inspired by the rusting locos in Barry scrapyard.

FACING PAGE TOP In the summer of 1988, it was was planned for GWR No 7828 *Odney Manor* to go on loan to the Gwili Railway in West Wales. En route, on Wednesday 11 May, the locomotive called into Barry scrapyard on its low-loader for a publicity event. Here owner Ken Ryder and the previous owner, Dai Woodham, shake hands on the locomotive's footplate in the scrapyard. *John Woodham collection*

FACING PAGE BOTTOM Ex-Barry scrapyard GWR No 4930 *Hagley Hall*, coupled to No 7029 *Clun Castle*, is prepared at Cardiff Canton diesel depot for the 6 July 1985 'Western Stalwart' main-line rail tour. *Peter Brabham*

TOP At the request of South Glamorgan Council, GWR locomotive No 5538 was donated by Woodham Brothers for display on Barry seafront in 1992. In fact, No 5538 and sister No 5532 had both been dismantled at the Dean Forest Railway and many parts were swapped before the cosmetic restoration of No 5538 took place. This diorama lasted five years before it was dismantled and the locomotive was transferred to the nearby Barry Island Railway Heritage Centre. The locomotive is now back at the Dean Forest Railway, so no permanent tribute to Barry scrapyard presently exists in the town. *Peter Brabham*

ABOVE GWR No 9629 was purchased in 1981 for cosmetic display outside the then newly built Holiday Inn in central Cardiff in 1986. It was best viewed at night, as it had a fabricated boiler and dome that did not bear close inspection. In 1995 the locomotive was given to the Blaenavon Railway, where it is awaiting a replacement boiler for future restoration to steam. *Peter Brabham*

Immaculate GWR 'Castle' No 5080 *Defiant* stands in Newport station waiting for a rail tour in 1990, inspected by a lone young trainspotter. No 5080 was originally named *Ogmore Castle* when built in 1939, but renamed in 1941 after the Second World War aircraft. *Defiant* was based at Cardiff Canton for much of its working life, and later, during the early 1960s, at Llanelli, West Wales, being withdrawn for scrapping in 1963. Given the locomotive's ransacked state after 11 years standing in Woodham Brothers' scrapyard, it was originally purchased for spare parts for classmate No 7029 *Clun Castle*, which had been purchased direct from BR at the end of steam. Thankfully it was decided to restore *Defiant* in its own right, and it is a fine tribute to the restoration engineers at Tyseley, Birmingham, that it was restored to main-line condition by June 1988. Since its ten-year certification expired in 1997, it has stood only as a museum exhibit at the Buckinghamshire Railway Centre. *Peter Brabham*

TOP During a visit to the Blaenavon Railway on 15 September 2008, GWR 0-6-2T ex-Barry scrapyard 'Taffytank' No 5619 brings back memories of the South Wales valleys in the late 1950s. *Peter Brabham*

ABOVE In June 2007, ex-Barry scrapyard 0-6-2T 'Taffytank' No 5643 paid a short visit to the Vale of Glamorgan Railway at Barry. Here the locomotive is seen on the causeway bridge (originally built over the docks sidings) only a few metres above the site where it rusted away in the scrapyard from 1963 to 1971.
Peter Brabham

TOP In May 2003, on a perfect cold bright spring morning, GWR No 5029 *Nunney Castle* blasts along the South Wales main line westward at Llanwern with, for once, a suitable full-liveried set of BR chocolate and cream coaches. *Peter Brabham*

ABOVE On St David's Day (1 March) 2007, GWR 'Castle' class No 5051 *Earl Bathurst* hauls a St David's Day special from Swansea to Paddington, captured at 8.30 in the morning going full tilt eastbound along the South Wales main line at St George's in the Vale of Glamorgan on its journey to London. The locomotive has also run in preservation under its alternative original name of *Drysllwyn Castle*. *Peter Brabham*

ABOVE There was great excitement back in April 1996 when *Taw Valley* was to run over the Vale of Glamorgan line to Swansea. The locomotive is seen here working hard up the gradient over the magnificent Porthkerry Viaduct in western Barry. Unfortunately soon after this shot was taken the locomotive was failed at Bridgend with a cracked spring. The rough riding over the then freight-only VoG track was given the blame.
Peter Brabham

LEFT On 28 May 2005, 'Thomas the Tank Engine' visited the Vale of Glamorgan Railway at Barry Island. The locomotive is in fact LMS No 47298, which was rescued from Barry scrapyard in 1974 for preservation at Southport. It returned to steam in 1979, but since 1983 has been based at Llangollen, visiting many heritage lines to entertain children and parents in its 'Thomas' guise. In 2012, No 47298 was put up for sale.
Peter Brabham

LEFT In the early years of main-line running in the late 1970s/early 1980s, preserved steam locomotives were allowed on only a few selected routes, and the Newport-Hereford-Shrewsbury route was one of them. Ex-Barry scrapyard LMS 'Jubilee' class No 45690 *Leander* was a regular on the 'Welsh Marches Express' trains in the 1980s, as seen here at Ponthir north of Newport on 18 February 1984.
Andrew Wiltshire

GWR locomotives Nos 4965 *Rood Ashton Hall* and 4953 *Pitchford Hall* power a main-line special southbound though the Welsh borderlands at Abergavenny in September 2006. *Peter Brabham*

On 26 May 2007, No 71000 *Duke of Gloucester* speeds westwards along the South Wales main line near Bridgend. It is hard to believe that this magnificent locomotive was once in Barry scrapyard minus cylinders and tender. *Peter Brabham*

ABOVE In October 1991, BR Standard tank No 80080 returned to Barry. It had left Barry scrapyard in 1980 to be restored at the Midland Railway Centre, then in 1991 it ran a series of special trains on the South Wales valley lines system to commemorate the 150th anniversary of the Taff Vale Railway. The open foreground in this photograph is the site of the derelict coal sidings of No 2 Dock, which now form Barry's new access road, so this wide-angle shot is now lost. The impressive building behind the coaches is the magnificent offices of the Barry Docks & Railway Company. *Peter Brabham*

LEFT One weekend back in September 2001, BR Standard No 76079 ran a series of special trains in the South Wales valleys. Typically, for such an eagerly awaited event, the weather conditions were atrocious for photography as 76079 pulls away in the rain and gloom from Trehafod station, Rhondda Valley after picking up passengers who had visited the Rhondda Heritage Park. *Peter Brabham*

On 6 September 2009, ex-Barry scrapyard pannier tank No 9466 returned to Barry depot to mark the birth of the Cambrian Transport Barry tourist railway project. It is standing only a few hundred metres from where it was rescued in 1975 by **Dennis Howells.** *Peter Brabham*

LEFT On 30 August 2010, No 6024 *King Edward I* speeds along the South Wales main line eastbound out of Kidwelly hauling a special. *King Edward I* has been slightly modified in height for main-line running to avoid hitting any overbridges, and this is most visibly obvious in the cut-down safety valve cover. *Peter Brabham*

No 6024 *King Edward I* is seen at 8.30 in the morning at Cardiff Central (General) station on a 'Red Dragon' express to Paddington – is this 1962? The 'King' was scheduled to run a midweek St David's Day (1 March) main-line special in 1995, and the weather was perfect for steam photography with low morning sunshine and a dark thundery sky. *Peter Brabham*

ABOVE Another St David's Day steam special charter in 2012, No 6024 *King Edward I* was scheduled to haul a 'Help for Heroes' special from Paddington to Cardiff and return. It is seen trying to make up 38 minutes by blasting westbound along the South Wales fast line at Bishton level crossing east of Newport. *Peter Brabham*

FACING PAGE TOP In 2003, ex-Barry scrapyard GWR locomotive No 5029 *Nunney Castle* runs west up the gradient out of Barry in the late evening sunset towards Rhoose and Bridgend on the Vale of Glamorgan line, having passed within a few metres of where it stood rusting in the Top Yard in the late 1960s. *Peter Brabham*

FACING PAGE BOTOM In 1941, the UK War Department offered neutral Turkey 25 LMS 8F locomotives built by the North British Company of Glasgow, but only 18 actually made it to Turkey, as seven were lost at sea. In Turkey the 8F locomotives were known by railwaymen as 'Churchills', and examples were still working there into the 1980s. In 2010 two of the six remaining derelict examples, which had not moved for more than a decade, were acquired by the Churchill 8F Locomotive Company. The pair were towed 850 miles by rail from Sivas depot to Izmir, where they were shipped back to Portbury Dock. One, No 45170, went on display at Shildon Museum, while No 45166 went into store at Barry shed. In September 2011 it was brought out of the shed during the Barry festival for temporary display outside the old goods shed, and is captured here in full Barry scrapyard glory by the author using multiple-exposure digital HDR image processing, a long way in quality from the Kodak Instamatic photos taken at the same location nearly 40 years earlier. In November 2012 the '8F' locomotive No 45166/WD341 left Barry depot to be exported via Southampton Docks for cosmetic restoration at a new regional railway heritage centre being established in the Municipality of Be'er Sheva, Israel. *Peter Brabham*

Appendix 1

In the early days of locomotive preservation in the 1970s, Barry locomotives were purchased for use on specific heritage lines. Today there is far more mobility of locomotives between heritage lines and preservation centres, especially for gala events. Locomotives with mainline certification also roam around the UK hauling charter trains. This listing provides the best indication where specific locomotives are most likely to be found around the UK in 2013. Locomotives listed as 'Restored' indicate that at some after leaving Barry scrapyard the particular locomotive was restored to steam. However steam locomotives require a 10-year boiler insurance certification and regular maintenance overhauls. Therefore, many locomotives listed as 'Restored' may not be found working in steam today. These ex-Barry locomotives are often found on display as static museum exhibits or are dismantled in the works for their regular overhauls and boiler re-certifications.

Former Great Western Railway Designed Locomotives

GWR 0-6-0 Pannier tank engines

3612	Collett 5700	0-6-0PT	Totally dismantled for spare parts	
3738	Collett 5700	0-6-0PT	Restored	Great Western Society, Didcot
4612	Collett 5700	0-6-0PT	Restored	Bodmin & Wenford Railway
9466	Hawksworth 9400	0-6-0PT	Restored	Buckinghamshire Railway Centre, Quainton
9629	Collett 5700	0-6-0PT	Under Restoration	Pontypool & Blaenavon Railway
9681	Collett 5700	0-6-0PT	Restored	Dean Forest Railway
9682	Collett 5700	0-6-0PT	Restored	Chinnor & Princes Risborough Railway

GWR 0-6-2 tank engines

5619	Collett 5600	0-6-2T	Restored	Telford Steam Railway
5637	Collett 5600	0-6-2T	Restored	East Somerset Railway
5643	Collett 5600	0-6-2T	Restored	Ribble Steam Railway
5668	Collett 5600	0-6-2T	Under Restoration	Pontypool & Blaenavon Railway
6619	Collett 5600	0-6-2T	Restored	Kent & East Sussex Railway
6634	Collett 5600	0-6-2T	Under Restoration	Severn Valley Railway
6686	Collett 5600	0-6-2T	Unrestored	Barry Rail Depot
6695	Collett 5600	0-6-2T	Restored	Swanage Railway

GWR 2-6-2 small prairie tank engines

4561	Churchward 4500	2-6-2T	Restored	West Somerset Railway
4566	Churchward 4500	2-6-2T	Restored	Severn Valley Railway
4588	Churchward 4575	2-6-2T	Restored	Dartmouth Steam Railway, Paignton (stored for sale)
5521	Churchward 4575	2-6-2T	Restored	Dean Forest Railway Railway
5526	Churchward 4575	2-6-2T	Restored	South Devon Railway
5532	Churchward 4575	2-6-2T	Under Restoration	Llangollen Railway
5538	Churchward 4575	2-6-2T	Under Restoration	Dean Forest Railway
5539	Churchward 4575	2-6-2T	Unrestored	Llangollen Railway
5541	Churchward 4575	2-6-2T	Restored	Dean Forest Railway
5542	Churchward 4575	2-6-2T	Restored	Gloucestershire Warwickshire Railway
5552	Churchward 4575	2-6-2T	Restored	Bodmin & Wenford Railway
5553	Churchward 4575	2-6-2T	Restored	West Somerset Railway
5572	Churchward 4575	2-6-2T	Restored	Great Western Society, Didcot

GWR 2-6-2 large prairie tank engines

4110	Collett 5101	2-6-2T	Under Restoration	Birmingham Railway Museum, Tyseley
4115	Collett 5101	2-6-2T	Donor of parts for rebuild project	Great Western Society, Didcot
4121	Collett 5101	2-6-2T	Under Restoration	Birmingham Railway Museum, Tyseley
4141	Collett 5101	2-6-2T	Restored	Epping & Ongar Railway
4144	Collett 5101	2-6-2T	Restored	Great Western Society, Didcot
4150	Collett 5101	2-6-2T	Under Restoration	Severn Valley Railway
4160	Collett 5101	2-6-2T	Restored	West Somerset Railway
5164	Collett 5101	2-6-2T	Restored	Severn Valley Railway
5193	Collett 5101	2-6-2T	Restored conversion to a GWR tender locomotive	West Somerset Railway
5199	Collett 5101	2-6-2T	Restored	Llangollen Railway

GWR 2-8-0 tank locomotives

4247	Churchward 4200	2-8-0T	Restored	Bodmin & Wenford Railway
4248	Churchward 4200	2-8-0T	Cosmetic Restoration	Swindon STEAM Museum
4253	Churchward 4200	2-8-0T	Under Restoration	Kent & East Sussex Railway
4270	Churchward 4200	2-8-0T	Under Restoration	Gloucestershire Warwickshire Railway
4277	Churchward 4200	2-8-0T	Restored	Dartmouth Steam Railway, Paignton
5224	Churchward 4200	2-8-0T	Restored	Great Central Railway, Loughborough
5227	Churchward 4200	2-8-0T	Donor of parts for Rebuild project	Great Western Society, Didcot
5239	Churchward 4200	2-8-0T	Restored	Dartmouth Steam Railway, Paignton

GWR 2-8-2 tank locomotives

7200	Collett 7200	2-8-2T	Under Restoration	Buckinghamshire Railway Centre, Quainton
7202	Collett 7200	2-8-2T	Under Restoration	Great Western Society, Didcot
7229	Collett 7200	2-8-2T	Unrestored and dismantled	East Lancashire Railway

GWR 2-6-0 tender locomotives

5322	Churchward 4300	2-6-0	Restored	Great Western Society, Didcot
7325/ 9309	Churchward 4300	2-6-0	Restored	Severn Valley Railway

2-8-0 tender locomotives

2807	Churchward 2800	2-8-0	Restored	Gloucestershire Warwickshire Railway
2857	Churchward 2800	2-8-0	Restored	Severn Valley Railway
2859	Churchward 2800	2-8-0	Unrestored	Llangollen Railway
2861	Churchward 2800	2-8-0	Donor of parts for rebuild project	Great Western Society, Didcot
2873	Churchward 2800	2-8-0	Unrestored and dismantled	South Devon Railway
2874	Churchward 2800	2-8-0	Unrestored	West Somerset Railway
2885	Churchward 2884	2-8-0	Cosmetic Restoration	Birmingham Moor St Station
3802	Churchward 2884	2-8-0	Restored	Llangollen Railway
3803	Churchward 2884	2-8-0	Restored	Gloucestershire & Warwickshire Railway
3814	Churchward 2884	2-8-0	Under Restoration	North Yorkshire Moors Railway
3822	Churchward 2884	2-8-0	Restored	Great Western Society, Didcot
3845	Churchward 2884	2-8-0	Unrestored	Gloucestershire Warwickshire Railway
3850	Churchward 2884	2-8-0	Restored	West Somerset Railway
3855	Churchward 2884	2-8-0	Unrestored	East Lancashire Railway
3862	Churchward 2884	2-8-0	Under Restoration	Northampton & Lamport Railway

GWR 4-6-0 'Manor' class tender locomotives

7802	Collett 7800	4-6-0	Restored	Severn Valley Railway
7812	Collett 7800	4-6-0	Restored	Severn Valley Railway
7819	Collett 7800	4-6-0	Restored	Severn Valley Railway
7820	Collett 7800	4-6-0	Restored	West Somerset Railway
7821	Collett 7800	4-6-0	Restored	STEAM Swindon/West Somerset Railway
7822	Collett 7800	4-6-0	Restored	Llangollen Railway
7827	Collett 7800	4-6-0	Restored	Dartmouth Steam Railway, Paignton
7828	Collett 7800	4-6-0	Restored	West Somerset Railway

GWR 4-6-0 'Hall' class tender locomotives

4920	Collett 4900	4-6-0	Restored	South Devon Railway
4930	Collett 4900	4-6-0	Restored	Severn Valley Railway
4936	Collett 4900	4-6-0	Restored	Birmingham Railway Museum, Tyseley
4942	Collett 4900	4-6-0	Donor of parts for Rebuild project	Great Western Society, Didcot
4953	Collett 4900	4-6-0	Restored	Epping Ongar Railway
4979	Collett 4900	4-6-0	Unrestored	Appleby Station Heritage Centre
4965	Collett 4900	4-6-0	Restored	Mainline based at Birmingham Railway museum, Tyseley
5900	Collett 4900	4-6-0	Restored	Great Western Society, Didcot
5952	Collett 4900	4-6-0	Donor of parts for Rebuild project	Llangollen Railway
5967	Collett 4900	4-6-0	Unrestored	Northampton & Lamport Railway

5972	Collett 4900	4-6-0	Restored	Mainline Steam Specials – Based at West Coast Rail Co., Carnforth

GWR 4-6-0 'Modified Hall' class tender locomotives

6960	Hawksworth 6959	4-6-0	Restored	West Somerset Railway
6984	Hawksworth 6959	4-6-0	Under Restoration	Gloucestershire Warwickshire Railway
6989	Hawksworth 6959	4-6-0	Under Restoration	Buckinghamshire Railway Centre, Quainton
6990	Hawksworth 6959	4-6-0	Restored	Great Central Railway, Loughborough
7903	Hawksworth 6959	4-6-0	Restored	Gloucestershire Warwickshire Railway
7927	Hawksworth 6959	4-6-0	Donor of parts for rebuild project	

GWR 4-6-0 'Castle' class tender locomotives

5029	Collett 4073	4-6-0	Restored	Mainline – GWS Didcot
5043	Collett 4073	4-6-0	Restored	Mainline – based at Birmingham Railway museum, Tyseley
5051	Collett 4073	4-6-0	Restored	Great Western Society, Didcot
5080	Collett 4073	4-6-0	Restored	Buckinghamshire Railway Centre, Quainton
7027	Collett 4073	4-6-0	Unrestored	Crewe Heritage Centre

GWR 4-6-0 King class tender locomotives

6023	Collett 6000	4-6-0	Restored	Great Western Society, Didcot
6024	Collett 6000	4-6-0	Restored	Mainline – based at Bristol or West Somerset Railway

Former Southern Railway Designed Locomotives

SR 0-6-0 tender locomotive

30541	Maunsell Q	0-6-0	Restored	Bluebell Railway

SR 2-6-0 tender locomotives

31618	Maunsell U	2-6-0	Restored	Bluebell Railway
31625	Maunsell U	2-6-0	Restored	Mid Hants Railway
31638	Maunsell U	2-6-0	Restored	Bluebell Railway
31806	Maunsell U	2-6-0	Restored	Mid Hants Railway
31874	Maunsell N	2-6-0	Restored	Mid Hants Railway

SR 4-6-0 tender locomotives

30499	Urie S15	4-6-0	Under restoration	Mid Hants Railway
30506	Urie S15	4-6-0	Restored	Mid Hants Railway
30825	Maunsell S15	4-6-0	Dismantled	North Yorkshire Moors Railway
30828	Maunsell S15	4-6-0	Restored	Mid Hants Railway
30830	Maunsell S15	4-6-0	Unrestored	North Yorkshire Moors Railway
30841	Maunsell S15	4-6-0	Restored	North Yorkshire Moors Railway
30847	Maunsell S15	4-6-0	Restored	Bluebell Railway

SR 4-6-2 Bulleid 'West Country'/'Battle of Britain' tender locomotives

34007	Original West Country	4-6-2	Restored	Mid Hants Railway
34010	Rebuilt West Country	4-6-2	Unrestored	Swanage Railway
34016	Rebuilt West Country	4-6-2	Restored	Mid Hants Railway
34027	Rebuilt West Country	4-6-2	Restored	Severn Valley Railway
34028	Rebuilt West Country	4-6-2	Restored	Swanage Railway
34039	Rebuilt West Country	4-6-2	Restored	Great Central Railway, Loughborough
34046	Rebuilt West Country	4-6-2	Restored	West Somerset Railway
34053	Rebuilt Battle of Britain	4-6-2	Restored	Severn Valley Railway
34058	Rebuilt Battle of Britain	4-6-2	Under restoration	Mid Hants Railway
34059	Rebuilt Battle of Britain	4-6-2	Restored	Bluebell Railway
34067	Original Battle of Britain	4-6-2	Restored	Mainline – Based at Southall, London
34070	Original Battle of Britain	4-6-2	Restored	Swanage Railway
34072	Original Battle of Britain	4-6-2	Restored	Swanage Railway
34073	Original Battle of Britain	4-6-2	Unrestored	East Lancashire Railway
34081	Original Battle of Britain	4-6-2	Restored	Nene Valley Railway, Peterborough
34092	Original West Country	4-6-2	Restored	Keighley & Worth Valley Railway
34101	Rebuilt West Country	4-6-2	Restored	North Yorkshire Moors Railway
34105	Original West Country	4-6-2	Restored	Mid Hants Railway

SR 4-6-2 Bulleid 'Merchant Navy' tender locomotives

35005	Merchant Navy	4-6-2	Restored	Eastleigh Works, Southampton
35006	Merchant Navy	4-6-2	Under restoration	Gloucestershire & Warwickshire Railway
35009	Merchant Navy	4-6-2	Unrestored	In Store – Bury, Lancashire
35010	Merchant Navy	4-6-2	Unrestored	Colne Valley Railway, Essex
35011	Merchant Navy	4-6-2	Under restoration	Sellindge, Kent
35018	Merchant Navy	4-6-2	Unrestored	West Coast Rail Co. Carnforth
35022	Merchant Navy	4-6-2	Unrestored	Southall Depot, London
35025	Merchant Navy	4-6-2	Under restoration	Sellindge, Kent
35027	Merchant Navy	4-6-2	Restored	Mainline Locomotive – based at Southall Depot
35029	Merchant Navy	4-6-2	Sectioned Cosmetic Restoration	National Railway Museum, York

Former London Midland & Scottish Railway Designed Locomotives

0-6-0 tank locomotives

47279	Fowler 3F Jinty	0-6-0T	Restored	Keighley & Worth Valley Railway
47298	Fowler 3F Jinty	0-6-0T	Restored	Llangollen Railway
47324	Fowler 3F Jinty	0-6-0T	Restored	East Lancashire Railway
47327	Fowler 3F Jinty	0-6-0T	Restored	Midland Railway Centre, Butterley
47357	Fowler 3F Jinty	0-6-0T	Restored	Midland Railway Centre, Butterley
47406	Fowler 3F Jinty	0-6-0T	Restored	Great Central Railway, Loughborough
47493	Fowler 3F Jinty	0-6-0T	Restored	Spa Valley Railway, Tunbridge Wells

2-6-2 tank locomotives

41312	Ivatt 2MT	2-6-2T	Restored	Mid Hants Railway
41313	Ivatt 2MT	2-6-2T	Unrestored	Isle of Wight Railway

0-6-0 tender locomotives

43924	Fowler (Midland) 4F	0-6-0	Restored	Keighley & Worth Valley Railway
44123	Fowler (Midland) 4F	0-6-0	Under Restoration	Avon Valley Railway, Bitton
44422	Fowler (Midland) 4F	0-6-0	Restored	Nene Valley Railway, Peterborough

2-6-0 tender locomotives

42765	Stanier 5FH Crab	2-6-0	Restored	East Lancashire Railway
42859	Stanier 5FH Crab	2-6-0	Unrestored dismantled	RAF Binbrook, Lincolnshire
42968	Stanier 5FS Mogul	2-6-0	Restored	Severn Valley Railway
46428	Ivatt 2MT	2-6-0	Unrestored	East Lancashire Railway
46447	Ivatt 2MT	2-6-0	Under Restoration	East Somerset Railway
46512	Ivatt 2MT	2-6-0	Restored	Strathspey Railway, Aviemore, Scotland
46521	Ivatt 2MT	2-6-0	Restored	Great Central Railway, Loughborough
44901	Stanier 5P5F	4-6-0	Unrestored	Gloucestershire Warwickshire Railway
45163	Stanier 5P5F	4-6-0	Under Restoration	Colne Valley Railway, Essex
45293	Stanier 5P5F	4-6-0	Under Restoration	Colne Valley Railway, Essex
45337	Stanier 5P5F	4-6-0	Restored	East Lancashire Railway
45379	Stanier 5P5F	4-6-0	Restored	Mid Hants Railway
45491	Stanier 5P5F	4-6-0	Under Restoration	Midland Railway Centre, Butterley
45690	Stanier 5XP Jubilee	4-6-0	Restored	Mainline – based at West Coast Railway Co., Carnforth
45699	Stanier 5XP Jubilee	4-6-0	Under Restoration	West Coast Railway Co., Carnforth

2-8-0 tender locomotives

48151	Stanier 8F	2-8-0	Restored	West Coast Railway Co., Carnforth
48173	Stanier 8F	2-8-0	Under Restoration	Churnet Valley Railway, Staffordshire
48305	Stanier 8F	2-8-0	Restored	Great Central Railway, Loughborough
48431	Stanier 8F	2-8-0	Restored	Keighley & Worth Valley Railway
48518	Stanier 8F	2-8-0	Donor of parts for Rebuild project	
48624	Stanier 8F	2-8-0	Restored	Churnet Valley Railway, Staffordshire
53808	Fowler 7F	2-8-0	Restored	West Somerset Railway
53809	Fowler 7F	2-8-0	Restored	North Yorkshire Moors Railway

Former London & North Eastern Railway Designed locomotive
4-6-0 tender locomotive

61264	Thompson B1	4-6-0	Restored	Barrow Hill, Chesterfield, Derbyshire

British Railways Standard Designed locomotives
2-6-4 tank locomotives

80064	Class 4MT	2-6-4T	Restored	Bluebell Railway
80072	Class 4MT	2-6-4T	Restored	Llangollen Railway
80078	Class 4MT	2-6-4T	Restored	Swanage Railway
80079	Class 4MT	2-6-4T	Restored	Severn Valley Railway
80080	Class 4MT	2-6-4T	Restored	Midland Railway Centre, Butterley
80097	Class 4MT	2-6-4T	Under Restoration	East Lancashire Railway
80098	Class 4MT	2-6-4T	Restored	Midland Railway Centre, Butterley
80100	Class 4MT	2-6-4T	Under Restoration	Bluebell Railway
80104	Class 4MT	2-6-4T	Restored	Swanage Railway
80105	Class 4MT	2-6-4T	Restored	Bo'ness & Kinneil Railway, Falkirk
80135	Class 4MT	2-6-4T	Restored	North Yorkshire Moors Railway
80136	Class 4MT	2-6-4T	Restored	Crewe Heritage Centre
80150	Class 4MT	2-6-4T	Unrestored	Mid Hants Railway
80151	Class 4MT	2-6-4T	Restored	Bluebell Railway

2-6-0 Class 2 tender locomotives

78018	Class 2MT	2-6-0	Under Restoration	Great Central Railway
78019	Class 2MT	2-6-0	Restored	Severn Valley Railway
78022	Class 2MT	2-6-0	Restored	Keighley & Worth Valley Railway
78059	Class 2MT	2-6-0	Under restoration conversion to '84000' class tank	Bluebell Railway

2-6-0 Class 4 tender locomotives

76017	Class 4MT	2-6-0	Restored	Mid Hants Railway
76077	Class 4MT	2-6-0	Unrestored	Gloucestershire & Warwickshire Railway
76079	Class 4MT	2-6-0	Restored	North Yorkshire Moors Railway
76084	Class 4MT	2-6-0	Restored	North Norfolk Railway

4-6-0 Class 4 tender locomotives

75014	Class 4MT	4-6-0	Restored	Dartmouth Steam Railway, Paignton
75069	Class 4MT	4-6-0	Restored	Severn Valley Railway
75078	Class 4MT	4-6-0	Restored	Keighley & Worth Valley Railway
75079	Class 4MT	4-6-0	Under Restoration	Mid Hants Railway

4-6-0 Class 5MT tender locomotives

73082	Class 5MT	4-6-0	Restored	Bluebell Railway
73096	Class 5MT	4-6-0	Restored	Mid Hants Railway
73129	Class 5MT	4-6-0	Restored	Midland Railway Centre, Butterley
73156	Class 5MT	4-6-0	Under Restoration	Great Central Railway, Loughborough

4-6-2 Class 8P tender locomotive

71000	Class 8P	4-6-2	Restored	East Lancashire Railway

2-10-0 Class 9F tender locomotives

92134	Class 9F	2-10-0	Under Restoration	Crewe Heritage Centre
92207	Class 9F	2-10-0	Under Restoration	Shillingstone Sta., Dorset
92212	Class 9F	2-10-0	Restored	Mid Hants Railway
92214	Class 9F	2-10-0	Restored	North Yorkshire Moors Railway
92219	Class 9F	2-10-0	Unrestored	Midland Railway Centre Butterley
92240	Class 9F	2-10-0	Restored	Bluebell Railway
92245	Class 9F	2-10-0	Unrestored	Barry Rail Depot

Appendix 2

Map of ex-Barry Locomotive UK locations as per Summer 2012

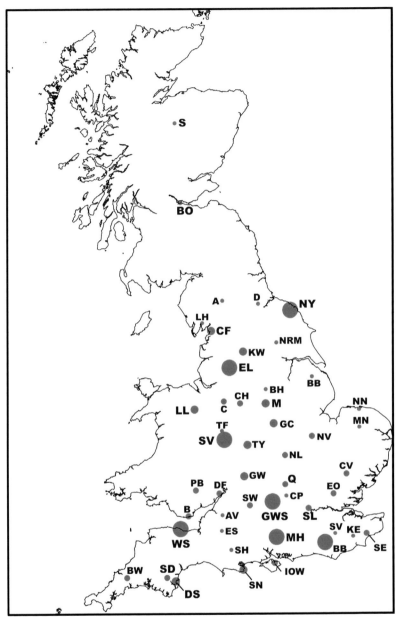

Site Index (size of circle is proportional to number of locomotives present)

Appleby Station Heritage Centre A
Avon Valley Railway, Bitton AV
Barrow Hill, Chesterfield, Derbyshire BH
Barry Rail Depot B
Birmingham Railway Museum, Tyseley TY
Bluebell Railway BB
Bodmin & Wenford Railway BW
Bo'ness & Kinneil Railway, Falkirk BO
Buckinghamshire Railway Centre, Quainton Q
Carnforth CF
Chinnor & Princes Risborough Railway CP
Churnet Valley Railway, Staffordshire CH
Colne Valley Railway, Essex CV
Crewe Heritage Centre C
Darlington North Road Works D
Dartmouth Steam Railway, Paignton DS
Dean Forest Railway DF
East Lancashire Railway EL
East Somerset Railway ES
Epping & Ongar Railway EO
Gloucestershire & Warwickshire Railway GW
Great Central Railway, Loughborough GC
Great Western Society, Didcot GWS
Isle of Wight Railway IoW
Keighley & Worth Valley Railway KW
Kent & East Sussex Railway KE
Lakeside & Haverthwaite Railway, Cumbria LH
Llangollen Railway LL
Mid Hants Railway MH
Midland Railway Centre, Butterley M
Mid Norfolk Railway MN
National Railway Museum, York NRM
Nene Valley Railway, Peterborough NV
Northampton & Lamport Railway NL
North Norfolk Railway NN
North Yorkshire Moors Railway NY
Pontypool & Blaenavon Railway PB
RAF Binbrook, Lincolnshire BB
Sellindge, Kent SE
Severn Valley Railway SV
Shillingstone Railway Project, Dorset SH
Southall SL
South Devon Railway SD
Spa Valley Railway, Tunbridge Wells SV
Strathspey Railway, Aviemore, Scotland S
Swanage Railway SN
Swindon STEAM Museum SW
Telford Steam Railway TF
West Somerset Railway WS

Bibliography

Books

The following is a list of very useful publications consulted for research in the compilation of this book :

A pictorial record of Great Western locomotives, J.H.Russell, OPC, 1978.
A pictorial record of Southern locomotives, J.H.Russell, Foulis-OPC, 1991.
A regional history of the railways of Great Britain : vol. 12 - South Wales, D.S.M. Barrie, David St John Thomas, 1980.
Barry No.1 Dock : The building of a giant, Archive: The quarterly journal for British industrial and transport history. Issue 40, Dec 2003.
Barry a centenary book, Ed. D. Moore, Barry Centenary Book Ltd, 1984.
Barry Docks & Railways : 1865 & 1876: the schemes that failed, I.W. Prothero, Pub. author, 1994.
Barry Island & Cold Knap, B.A.Thomas, Einion Books, 2010.
Barry scrapyard the preservation miracle, A. Warren, Guild Publishing, 1988.
Bluebell Locomotives as they were, R.Inns & J. Scott-Morgan, Midland Publishing Ltd., 1996.
British Railways bridges & viaducts, M.Smith, Ian Allan, 1994.
Cardiff and the Marquesses of Bute, J. Davies, University of Wales, 1981.
Forgotten Railways of South Wales, J. Page, David & Charles, 1979.
Graveyard of steam, B. Handley, George Allan & Unwin Ltd, 1979.
Keighley & Worth Valley Railway Locomotives as they were, T. Heavyside, Midland Publishing Limited, 1996.
Peto's register of Great Western Railway Locomotives Vol.1 King 4-6-0s, B.Peto, Irwell Press, 1995.
Rails in the valleys, J. Page, Guild Publishing London, 1989.
Rails to prosperity – the Barry and after 1884 to 1984, B.J.Miller, Regional Publications, 1984.
Railways of Great Britain, Colonel M.H. Cobb, Ian Allan, 2011.
Rhondda coal Cardiff gold, R. Watson, Merton Priory Press Ltd, 1997.
Severn Valley Locomotives as they were, T. Ferris, Midland Publishing Ltd., 1995.
South Wales Ports, British Transport Commission, 1948.
Steam in South Wales: vol.3 main line and the docks, M.Hale, OPC, 1982.
The British steam railway locomotive vol.2 from 1925 to 1965, O.S.Nock, Ian Allan 1966.
Images of Barry scrapyard, R. Hardingham, Waterfront, 1999.
Jowett's railway atlas, A.Jowett, Guild Publishing, 1989.
Steam for scrap - the complete story, Ed. A. Earnshaw, Atlantic, 1993.
The Barry album, Peter Nicholson, Pub. author, 1981.
The Barry Railway, D.S.M.Barrie, Oakwood Press, 1962.
The Barry story including the Barry list 10th edition, M. Beckett & R. Hardingham, Kingfisher Productions, 2010.
The Barry locomotive phenomenon, F. Blake & P. Nicholson, Foulis-OPC, 1987.

The railways of Wales circa 1900, G.B.Jones & D.Dunstone, Gomer, 2000.
The USA 756th RSB at Newport (Ebbw Junction), E.R.Mountford, Oakwood Press, 1989.
The Vale of Glamorgan Railway, C. Chapman, Oakwood Press, 1998.
The Waterfront Barry : the redevelopment of no.1 dock, D.A. Scott, in Urban Geology of Wales I, Geological series no.23, National Museum of Wales, 2004.
Top Sawyer (the life of David Davies), I.Bulmer-Thomas, Longmans, Green & Co.Ltd., 1938.
Welsh Valleys Cardiff to Pontypridd, V.Mitchell & K.Smith, Middleton Press, 2011.
Welsh Railways a photographer's view, D.Dunstone, Gomer, 2002.
71000 Duke of Gloucester the impossible dream, P. King, Ian Allan Ltd, 1987.

Various useful articles

Magazine articles on particular ex-Barry scrapyard locomotives appear regularly in the many and various monthly railway magazine publications, there are far too many to list here. The following is a short list of particularly useful articles on the Barry Railway, Docks and Woodham Brother's scrapyard:

Barry the curtain comes down, D.Wilcock, Steam Railway no.111, July 1989.
Barry Dock and Railways near Cardiff, Mr J Woolfe Barry et al., The Engineer, March 4th 1887.
Barry Island excursion traffic, J. Hodge, Steam Days, Redgauntlet, February 1997.
Barry Island excursion traffic, S.L. Jacobs, Trains Illustrated summer annual no.3, Ian Allan, 1960.
Barry Rescue, R.Adley MP, Railway World, Ian Allan, February 1990.
Demolishing the Rhymney branch of the Barry Railway, The Railway Magazine, December 1937.
Nightmare! Dai Woodham tells the other story, D.Wilcock, Steam Railway no.1, June 1979.
Pontypridd and the Rhondda Valleys, R. Malyn, Steam Days, Redgauntlet, February 2006.

Websites

Up to date details, histories and the current state of restoration of the ex-Barry scrapyard engines can be found on websites of the heritage railway lines and locomotive preservation societies. The following websites were found particularly useful in cross-checking information for this book:

www.railuk.info
www.br-steam-allocations.co.uk
www.greatwestern.org.uk